The book tackles a vital problem in our country. While there are many efforts to address inequality among educational and health professionals, we often operate as if health does not affect education and education does not affect health. Nadine Finigan-Carr has moved the conversation forward by compiling the evidence of the health/education link.

Thomas LaVeist, PhD
Chairman of the Department of Health Policy and Management,
George Washington University,
Milken Institute School of Public Health

Dr. Finigan-Carr assembled groundbreaking research, thoughtful analysis, and a compassionate understanding to build a compelling case for *Linking Health and Education for African American Students' Success*. Both intellectually stimulating and easy to read, *Linking Health* gives a comprehensive picture of the health-related antecedents to positive educational outcome. The book is serious and provocative with describing critical health issues, yet hopeful and forward-thinking in presenting a vision for healthy educational environments for African Americans.

Ivory A. Toldson, PhD
Director of Quality Education for Minorities,
Professor, Howard University,
Editor-in-Chief, The Journal of Negro Education,
Contributing Education Editor, TheRoot.com

Health outcomes are intertwined with educational outcomes. This book describes this truth for African American children but more importantly suggests a path forward.

Tina L. Cheng, MD, MPH
Director of the Department of Pediatrics,
Johns Hopkins University School of Medicine,
Pediatrician in Chief, Johns Hopkins Children's Center

Racism has left an ugly stain on America's history, and it has created structural inequalities, which have affected African American students' educational and health outcomes. *Linking Health and Education for African American Students' Success* challenges those issues and provides compelling evidence for the causal role that *educationally relevant health disparities* play amongst African American students. With an unparalleled depth of insight and clarity of voice, Dr. Finigan-Carr's book must be a fundamental part of school reform.

LaMarr Darnell Shields, PhD
Change Agent and Author,
What I Learned in the Midst of KAOS: The Making of an Ubuntu Teacher

Linking Health and Education for African American Students' Success

Linking Health and Education for African American Students' Success

Edited by

Nadine M. Finigan-Carr

Routledge
Taylor & Francis Group

LONDON AND NEW YORK

First published 2017 by Routledge

2 Park Square, Milton Park, Abingdon, Oxfordshire OX14 4RN
52 Vanderbilt Avenue, New York, NY 10017

Routledge is an imprint of the Taylor & Francis Group, an informa business

First issued in paperback 2019

Library of Congress Cataloging-in-Publication Data

Names: Finigan-Carr, Nadine, editor.
Title: Linking health and education for African American students' success / edited by Nadine Finigan-Carr.
Description: Abingdon, Oxon ; New York, NY : Routledge, 2017. | Includes bibliographical references and index.
Identifiers: LCCN 2016035317 | ISBN 9781498767064 (hardback) | ISBN 9781315367361 (ebook)
Subjects: | MESH: Health Status | African Americans--education | Child | Adolescent | Students | Socioeconomic Factors | United States
Classification: LCC RA448.5.N4 | NLM WA 300 AA1 | DDC 362.1089/96073--dc23
LC record available at https://lccn.loc.gov/2016035317

ISBN: 978-1-4987-6706-4 (hbk)
ISBN: 978-0-367-22414-1 (pbk)

Contents

PART II
Interventions with an impact on both health
behaviors and educational outcomes

Acknowledgments

The process of completing this book has been an incredible journey filled with ebbs and flows. I am tremendously grateful for the support of so many in this endeavor. First, I would like to thank my husband, Sylvester, whose love and encouragement have allowed me to be an academic with all that entails. My number one motivator and coach has been my son, Jahid! I appreciate them for giving me the space and time to write, edit, and compile this book. My family has been my first and favorite cheerleaders—Pop, Nicole, Jessica, Darnell, and Dorrein!

I have been tremendously blessed by the guidance and support of several women, sister friends, and confidantes. Thank you to my bestie, Stephanie Taylor, for always being there with the wine! Dana Jackson and Ndaneh Smart-Smith, thank you for the working mom advice. I'm grateful for the PhDivas (Natasha, Nanlesta, and Zupenda) who remind me that unicorns do exist. I'm indebted to SCOS (Kantahyanee, Melissa, Theda, Tanya, and Wendy) for being my sisters in the academy. My sorors of Alpha Kappa Alpha Sorority, Inc., have been there even when I didn't realize I needed them and I appreciate that. Thanks to the Chicas, especially Aurelia, Cinneen, Aisha, Dee, and Sherrillyn, for providing me with space to vent.

I must offer high praise for the book's contributors for such informative chapters and for promoting the goals and objectives of this book. Another thank you goes out to my social media family at Twitter.com/doctornayaka (you know who you are) for sharing with me resources on a daily basis that have been influential in reminding me of why writing this book was important. Most especially, I would like to thank Lara Zoble, my editor at Routledge, for her guidance, patience, and support for this project from day one.

Finally, I would like to dedicate this book to my mother, Annette Angela Finigan Nosiles. She was my first supporter in life and with this book. Right as I was finishing it up, she transitioned to be with the ancestors. I'd like to think that she is smiling down upon me as I share this knowledge with you all.

Editor

Nadine M. Finigan-Carr, PhD, is a prevention research scientist focused on the application of behavioral and social science perspectives to research contemporary health problems, especially those that disproportionately affect people of color. Her scholarship is grounded in theories and methods found primarily in the field of health behavior change among individuals and the environments (social, informational, psychological) that support or impede chronic disease prevention or management, injury, and violence. More specifically, she has focused on adolescent risk behaviors and their determinants.

Finigan-Carr began her career as a classroom teacher where she quickly realized that teaching was more than being aware of the educational needs of her students but also involved their physical and mental health needs. Currently, Finigan-Carr is a research assistant professor at the University of Maryland, School of Social Work. In this position she has two main research projects at both the state and federal levels designed to intervene with system-involved youth—those in foster care or the juvenile justice system, for example. These youth have a double vulnerability: adolescence, a critical stage marked by increased risk for negative social and behavioral outcomes including aggression and sexual risk behaviors; and being removed from their families of origin.

Finigan-Carr is married to Sylvester Carr, a retired Marine. Together they have one biological son, Jahid, and one adopted son, Dorrein. She is a Silver Star member of Alpha Kappa Alpha Sorority, Incorporated, having served the sisterhood for more than 25 years. She serves on the board of the Healthy Teen Network and is an active member of the Society for Prevention Research and the American Public Health Association.

Contributors

Jessika H. Bottiani, PhD, MPH, is a postdoctoral fellow at the Curry School of Education, University of Virginia. Bottiani has research expertise in the collection and analysis of observational data in schools as part of large-scale randomized controlled trials, including the Double Check project funded by the Institute of Education Sciences, which integrates positive behavioral interventions and supports with coaching and professional development to address the discipline gap.

Catherine P. Bradshaw, PhD, MEd, is a professor and the associate dean for Research and Faculty Development at the Curry School of Education at the University of Virginia. She is also the deputy director of the Johns Hopkins Center for the Prevention of Youth Violence funded by the Centers for Disease Control and Prevention (CDC), codirector of the Johns Hopkins Center for Prevention and Early Intervention funded by the National Institute of Mental Health (NIMH). She collaborates on federally funded research projects examining bullying and school climate; the development of aggressive and problem behaviors; and the design, evaluation, and implementation of evidence-based prevention programs in schools.

Lawrence Brown, PhD, is an assistant professor in the School of Community Health and Policy at Morgan State University. He conducts research into the impact of masculinity on Black men's health and health behaviors along with the effects of displacement and gentrification on African American communities. He is engaged in Baltimore communities as an activist for equitable redevelopment.

Marino A. Bruce, PhD, MSRC, MDiv, CRC, is a professor of sociology and criminal justice at Jackson State University whose research focuses on the intersection of race, gender, class, age, faith, behavior, and their implications for social and health outcomes. His current program of research focuses on specifying social, psychological, spiritual, and behavioral factors impacting the health of African American boys and young men.

Shanda C. Crowder, EdD, MEd, is the director of the Positive Schools Center at the University of Maryland School of Social Work; a project created to partner with Maryland school districts to help improve school climate, and reduce out-of-school suspensions and expulsions of students of color and students with disabilities. Over the course of her career she has developed organizational structures; implemented educational programs for youth and families; and has provided leadership and support to school-based and government organizations.

Katrina J. Debnam, PhD, MPH, is an assistant scientist in the Department of Mental Health at Johns Hopkins Bloomberg School of Public Health. She has expertise in mixed-methods research, including hierarchical linear modeling, and the conduct and analysis of data from focus groups and interviews. Her research interests include health disparities, adolescent dating violence prevention, school culture, and faith-based programs for positive youth development.

Ramon B. Goings, PhD, is an assistant professor of educational leadership at Loyola University Maryland. His research interests are centered on the following: disrupting the deficit narratives about African American students generally and males specifically; investigating the resilience of nontraditional students of color in higher education; and investigating the preparation and professional experiences of urban educators.

Derek M. Griffith, PhD, is the director of the Institute for Research on Men's Health and an associate professor of Medicine, Health and Society at Vanderbilt University. Trained in clinical-community psychology and public health, he uses mixed methods to inform and evaluate interventions to improve African American men's eating practices and physical activity in cancer and diabetes outcomes.

Stacey Houston II, MA, is a third-year doctoral student in the Department of Sociology at Vanderbilt University. His research interests include the sociology of education, quantitative methodology, diversity, higher education, and teaching and learning.

Sean Joe, PhD, holds joint positions as the associate dean for faculty and research and the Benjamin E. Youngdahl Professor of Social Development at Washington University in St. Louis' George Warren Brown School of Social Work. He is a nationally recognized authority on suicidal behavior among African Americans.

Brad Lian, PhD, is an associate professor at Mercer University with a joint appointment in the Department of Community Medicine in the School of Medicine and the Department of Public Health in the College of Health Professions. His research interests revolve around poverty, adolescent development, and community assessment.

Theda Rose, PhD, is an assistant professor at the University of Maryland School of Social Work. Her research interests include factors that promote mental health and prevent mental disorders among adolescents and the development, implementation, and evaluation of effective mental health interventions for Black adolescents, particularly in school settings.

Camika Royal, PhD, is an assistant professor of Urban Education at Loyola University Maryland. Her research interests are the social and political context of school reform policies, urban educator efficacy and resilience, critical race theory, and historical foundations of schooling. Royal also writes about contemporary education issues, and she has been a recurring education contributor to Al Jazeera America TV and the web show *Huff Post Live*.

Wendy E. Shaia, EdD, MSW, is the executive director of the Social Work Community Outreach Service (SWCOS), a center in the University of Maryland School of Social Work. She has more than 20 years of experience developing, implementing, and leading organizations and programs. Most recently, Shaia worked as a strategic planner for the Department of Defense, where she developed strategies around equal employment opportunity and diversity.

Tanya L. Sharpe, PhD, is an associate professor at the University of Maryland, School of Social Work. Her research is centered on developing research and services for African Americans who are surviving the homicide of a loved one. Sharpe is experienced in the design and implementation of community-based violence prevention and intervention programs that utilize culturally sensitive methods.

Roland J. Thorpe Jr., PhD, is an assistant professor in the Department of Health, Behavior and Society, and founding director of the Program for Research on Men's Health in the Center for Health Disparities Solutions at the Johns Hopkins Bloomberg School of Public Health. He is a social epidemiologist whose research focuses on the association of how social determinants of health impact health and functional outcomes among men across the life course.

Larry J. Walker, EdD, is an educational consultant who most recently served as a research fellow in the School of Graduate Studies at Morgan State University. His research examines the impact trauma has on the academic performance and socioemotional functioning of minority students in PreK–16 settings.

Introduction

Efforts to understand academic achievement and success for African American students require complex yet nuanced perspectives. On the one hand, significant attention has been directed to examining the adequacy of the school environment, that is, having appropriate educational resources and motivated and talented teachers, to promote academic success in all children and even more so for African American youth given observations about disparate academic performance, disproportionate representation of these students in special education, and lower rates of high school graduation and college matriculation. On the other hand, questions have been raised about school readiness, academic self-efficacy, and the motivation that African American students and their families bring to the educational process. Both of these canons reside in a United States societal cauldron that begins with the enslavement of the ancestors of African Americans, the challenges of transcending a period of chattel slavery post its formal end, the Jim Crow era, and the violence of integration to the modern era.

African American students encounter myriad academic, economic, and social barriers. For instance, poverty, health, and income disparities contribute to educational gaps between White and African American students. Unfortunately, African American students from underserved communities are more likely to be exposed to traumatic events in comparison to other subgroups including Asians, Hispanics, and Whites. Environmental factors including community, familial relationships, and school culture affect student outcomes. Students exposed to traumatic events are more likely to exhibit maladaptive behaviors including self-injury and early drug and alcohol abuse. Children and adolescents do not have the coping skills to overcome a singular or continuous traumatic event. Thus, schools have to ensure that school administrators, teachers, and auxiliary staff have access to professional development opportunities. Early identification is the key to preventing long-term psychological and physical problems. School districts have to screen all students to ensure victims of primary and secondary trauma have access to comprehensive mental health support services.

Educational theorists, practitioners, and policy makers have sought with varied motivation to identify and understand factors influencing resilience in academic performance for marginalized demographic groups in the United States (American Psychological Association, 2008). Often missing from these efforts, however, are considerations of the role of an individual's or community's public health status and the intersection of this status with some of the approaches identified earlier. Specifically, we assert it is a limiting approach that focuses on school resources and individual and familial characteristics absent an intentional consideration of the influence of health status. There is a substantive body of work that speaks directly to how physical and mental health influence academic performance and thus success. Simply put, those who experience positive health physically and mentally are better positioned to learn and experience a higher quality of life.

The purpose of *Linking Health and Education for African American Students' Success* is to examine the intersection of education and public health and its subsequent impact on the well-being of African American students in the United States. The chapters within examine the factors in their lives that have an impact on both the education and health status of these students, as well as programs and interventions that have an effect.

Part I: Health behaviors and educational outcomes

In the first part, we examine health behaviors and risks, and their impact on educational outcomes of African American students. The structural inequalities that lead to reduced academic attainment mirror the social determinants of health. Education is one of the most powerful determinants of health, and disparities in educational achievement as a result of structural inequalities closely track disparities in health. These disparities lead to both substandard health care and reduced academic attainment among children from underserved minorities in the United States, especially African Americans. This part discusses how this may result in children with poorer mental health outcomes, higher school-dropout rates, increased risks of arrests and incarceration, higher rates of chronic diseases and mortality, and overall diminished opportunities for success.

The extant literature has examined the ways children and youth respond to various stressors. The adaptation that occurs in the face of stressors often results in negative outcomes, such as poorer academic performance. Therefore, the presence of stressors results in children being labeled "at risk" for academic failure. Positive outcomes for individuals in the face of stressors have typically been framed within resilience theory. Resilience theory provides the opportunity to replace the negative outcomes in the presence of stressors with positive outcomes. It has recently surfaced as a critical piece of the stress theory puzzle. Contrary to previous beliefs, stressors do not function similarly for all groups of people, and scholars have found marked differences in response to stressors by both gender and race.

The chapters in this part delve into these stressors and their impact on the well-being of African American students. We begin with a comprehensive examination of the social determinants of health and its influence on resilience and academic success. Following this, we move on to the impact of trauma and racism on classroom behaviors. Then, we discuss the impact of family behaviors (including parental alcoholism), and student behaviors, aggression, and mental health on student achievement.

Part I chapter summaries

Chapter 1—A Dream Deferred: How Trauma Impacts the Academic Achievement of African American Youth by Larry J. Walker, EdD, and Ramon B. Goings, PhD, Morgan State University

This chapter examines the relationship between environmental factors (community, familial relationships, and school culture) and academic achievement for African American students in PreK–5 settings. Schools located in predominantly African American underserved communities continue to encounter a variety of obstacles, which hamper efforts to improve academic achievement. Addressing systemic problems requires a paradigm shift that focuses on socioemotional experiences of at-risk students located in urban, rural, or suburban communities. The chapter provides implications and recommendations for school reform.

Chapter 2—Racism as a Fundamental Determinant of Health for Black Boys by Roland J. Thorpe Jr., PhD, Johns Hopkins School of Public Health; Derek M. Griffith, PhD, Vanderbilt University; Marino A. Bruce, PhD, MSRC, MDiv, CRC, Jackson State University; and Lawrence Brown, PhD, Morgan State University

The factors affecting the educational achievement of Black males emerge long before they enter the classroom. Once born, racism-induced factors such as low birth weight, stress, and poverty have been shown to impair the brain function of children. Racial differences in maternal health as well as in children's health conditions may account for up to 25% of the racial gap in school readiness (Currie, 2005). Thus, racism produces a biological impact upon health directly connected to educational achievement later in life. Black boys are exposed to additional stressors and factors that are distinct from girls (i.e., masculinity and racist views of Black males). Inasmuch as racism's damage has been imposed on African American families, the solutions to address the preclassroom health and well-being of Black boys must be structural and multilevel in order to be effective in neutralizing racism's impact.

Chapter 3—Drinking and Learning While Black: The Effect of Family Problem Drinking on Children's Later Educational Attainment by Stacey Houston II, MA, Vanderbilt University

Families with an alcoholic member have been reported to have more stress, conflict, and negative effect than other families resulting in children with more risk for detrimental outcomes. However, a resilience theory framework has shown that there are some who experience superior adjustment in the face of these stressors. In this chapter, family stress theory and resilience theory help explain this phenomenon uncovered utilizing data from the National Longitudinal Survey of Youth and Young Adults. By estimating a series of multiple regression equations with interaction effects, it was found that there are African Americans who experience positive effects on educational attainment in the face of familial problem drinking. These results call into question the generalizability of stressors and the labeling of groups of children who experience these stressors as "at risk." By uncovering how this stressor functions differently for Whites and African Americans, this chapter questions the detrimental effects of stressors that often show up in large, aggregated samples. In doing so, it concurrently questions the labeling of certain groups of youths as "at risk." Though not concluding that certain groups of children should, indeed, face adversity, this study suggests that there may be characteristics of African American youth, namely, their reliance on extended kin networks, that could be capitalized upon to help foster resiliency and thereby decrease the dreaded achievement gap.

Chapter 4—Lifetime Mental Disorders and Education Experiences among Black Adolescents by Theda Rose, PhD, University of Maryland School of Social Work; Nadine M. Finigan-Carr, PhD, University of Maryland School of Social Work; and Sean Joe, PhD, University of Michigan School of Social Work

Behavioral problems that lead to school disciplinary action may reflect unmet needs with respect to mental health (Vincent, Grisso, Terry, & Banks, 2008), particularly among African American youth. Concurrently, prior research indicates that adolescents with mental health problems are more likely to experience poor academic functioning (Fergusson & Woodward, 2002; Ialongo, Edelsohn, & Kellam, 2001; Sznitman et al., 2011). This adverse relationship may be exacerbated among African American adolescents, who experience significant mental health problems (e.g., lifetime rates of 55% for any disorder including mood, anxiety, substance, and impulse disorders) (Kessler et al., 2012) and may report greater psychiatric problems and greater risk of comorbid mental health problems as compared to other racial/ethnic groups (Chen, Killeya-Jones, & Vega, 2005). This chapter describes the relationship between lifetime disorders and academic achievement among a national probability sample of Black adolescents. It also provides some information about these key constructs by gender.

Chapter 5—Community Violence, Adolescent Aggression, and Academic Achievement by Nadine M. Finigan-Carr, PhD, and Tanya L. Sharpe, PhD, University of Maryland School of Social Work

Adolescent aggression has been examined as a predictor for more serious forms of youth violent behavior. It is a complex phenomenon that has many determinants and yet serves multiple purposes. Taking a public health social work perspective, this chapter examines the disproportionate involvement of

African American youth in interpersonal violence due to aggressive behaviors. It also examines the social determinants of this involvement. After identifying and exploring the systemic factors related to this problem, the chapter explores relevant theories and their applicability in community-based interventions designed to prevent school violence and support academic achievement.

Part II: Interventions with an impact on both health behaviors and educational outcomes

Disparities in health status and access to health care among different racial, ethnic, and socioeconomic groups in the United States are a demonstrated fact. There is increased awareness about health disparities and attempts to reduce them. Likewise, there is abundant documented evidence of the marked educational gaps between different racial, ethnic, and socioeconomic groups. As shown in the prior section, the education gap begins before children go to kindergarten, and the gap widens as children continue their schooling. The end results are low achievement and high school-dropout rates among minority populations. Just like in the case of health, there have been numerous efforts to increase awareness about these problems, and attempts to reduce educational inequities. For both health disparities and educational inequities, initiatives have included designing, testing, and training on selective interventions, and also promoting progressive policy making at local, state, and national levels to attempt to reduce their impact on children and youth.

The chapters in this part discuss interventions and initiatives designed to address both health disparities and educational inequities and their impact on African American students' well-being. This part begins with an examination of the impact of school environments on student success. It then moves on to the impact of teacher behaviors on schools and student behaviors. As children and adolescents spend a substantial amount of their time outside of academic settings, the section ends with a look into afterschool activities, both formal and informal, and their potential for positive developmental outcomes among adolescents.

Part II chapter summaries

Chapter 6—Schools as Retraumatizing Environments by Wendy E. Shaia, EdD, MSW, and Shanda C. Crowder, EdD, MEd, University of Maryland School of Social Work

Many African American children in urban environments arrive at school experiencing the effects of complex trauma from their homes and communities, only to find that schools are environments where their trauma goes unrecognized and may be inadvertently exacerbated. In some school settings, the entire school community is exposed to trauma through a variety of events on a daily basis. In other cases, children experience new trauma in schools, as school staff attempt to discipline children for what they believe to be inappropriate behavior, as opposed to responses to the effects of trauma. Often, African American children experience more punitive consequences than do their peers of other races for the same behavior. This chapter will provide case examples of how children and school communities are retraumatized in schools, provide the context for their trauma, and offer potential solutions, using a trauma-informed perspective.

Chapter 7—Peace, Be Still: Black Educators Coping with Constant School Reforms in Philadelphia by Camika Royal, PhD, Loyola University Maryland

This chapter analyzes how Black educators responded to reform policies, racial politics, and the professional culture of the School District of Philadelphia (SDP), 1967–2007; and examines their resilience throughout this time period, including six superintendents and a state takeover. Three theories provide the lens through which this chapter is approached: critical race theory, narrative identity theory, and resilience theory. It examines Black educators' stories about SDP, its reforms and racialized issues and how they responded to them, and it extends Ladson-Billings and Tate's (1995) use of race as an analytic tool to understand Black educators' professional experiences within a racialized school district. Employing a qualitative, interpretive methodology, it is a phenomenological, historical ethnographic case study. Studies conducted of reform in urban school systems have focused on the reform efforts and the impact on students or students' academic performances, not the educators who stand between reforms and intended outcomes. Black educators' resilience and career mobility, as well as their responses to racialized practices and school reform policies based on local politics are an understudied, and therefore, not fully understood area of the politics of urban education (e.g., Cuban & Usdan, 2003; Tyack & Cuban, 1995). Black educators' relationships with one another and how they understood their jobs, the school district, and themselves in the district performing their jobs is lesser known. The extant literature has yet to demonstrate how the professional socialization and professional situations of Black educators are influenced by the policies and politics of the school and school district in which these educators work.

Chapter 8—Promoting Culturally Responsive Practice to Reduce Disparities in School Discipline among African American Students by Katrina J. Debnam, PhD, MPH, Johns Hopkins University School of Public Health; Jessika H. Bottiani, PhD, MPH, and Catherine P. Bradshaw, PhD, MEd, University of Virginia

The disproportionate representation of African American students in special education and disciplinary actions in the U.S. educational system is well documented. The inappropriate use of these actions among African American students can increase stigma and differential treatment by teachers, staff, and other students (Morrison & Skiba, 2001; Townsend, 2000). Furthermore, school suspension is a strong predictor of dropout and delayed graduation, and learning time missed as a result of suspensions and expulsions can lead to academic failure. Unfortunately, there are few empirically supported educational strategies that have been systematically tested and shown to reduce these inequities. The available research suggests that a schoolwide system of support, which includes data-based decision making and professional development for school staff on culturally responsive practice (including teaching and classroom management), holds promise as an effective strategy for reducing disproportionality. This chapter will discuss a promising framework called "Double Check" that was developed to promote teacher culturally responsive practice and student engagement to reduce disparities in school discipline among African American students.

Chapter 9—On Some Types and Consequences of After-School Activities in Low-Income Neighborhoods by Brad Lian, PhD, Mercer University, School of Medicine and Public Health

This chapter examines participation levels in several types of after-school activities and outcomes associated with adolescents growing up in low-income neighborhoods. Specifically, types and participation levels of four after-school activities are documented: participation in organized sports and clubs, working at a job, hanging out with friends, and hanging out alone at home. Using Mobile Youth Survey (MYS) data from 2008 to 2011, statistically significant gender and age differences were found on activity levels. For instance, males were found to be more involved in organized sports/clubs than females, although both genders reported being less involved as they age, with approximately 50% reporting no involvement between the ages of 16 and 18. Involvement in sports/clubs was generally positively associated with self-worth and is a protective factor against substance use for 16- to 18-year-olds. Working at a paid job and time spent hanging out with friends were also associated with several attitudes and behaviors among these youths. Understanding the nature and extent of after-school activities and the outcomes associated with them is critical if we are to develop or promote healthy activities aimed at improving adolescent health.

REFERENCES

American Psychological Association, Task Force on Resilience and Strength in Black Children and Adolescents. (2008). *Resilience in African American children and adolescents: A vision for optimal development.*

Chen, K. W., Killeya-Jones, L. A., & Vega, W. A. (2005). Prevalence and co-occurrence of psychiatric symptom clusters in the US adolescent population using DISC predictive scales. *Clinical Practice and Epidemiology in Mental Health, 1*(1), 22.

Cuban, L., & Usdan, M. (Eds.). (2003). *Powerful Reforms with Shallow Roots: Improving America's Urban Schools.* New York: Teachers College Press.

Currie, J. M. (2005). Health disparities and gaps in school readiness. *The Future of Children, 15*(1), 117–138.

Fergusson, D. M., & Woodward, L. J. (2002). Mental health, educational, and social role outcomes of adolescents with depression. *Archives of General Psychiatry, 59*(3), 225–231.

Ialongo, N. S., Edelsohn, G., & Kellam, S. G. (2001). A further look at the prognostic power of young children's reports of depressed mood and feelings. *Child Development, 72*(3), 736–747.

Kessler, R. C., Avenevoli, S., Costello, J., Georgiades, K., Green, J. G., Gruber, M. J., … Merikangas, K. M. (2012). Prevalence, persistence, and sociodemographic correlates of DSM-IV disorders in the national comorbidity survey replication adolescent supplement. *Archives of General Psychiatry, 69*, 372–380. doi:10.1001 /archgenpsychiatry.2011.160

Ladson-Billings, G., & Tate, W., IV. (1995). Toward a critical race theory of education. *The Teachers College Record, 97*(1), 47–68.

Morrison, G. M., & Skiba, R. (2001). Predicting violence from school misbehavior: Promises and perils. *Psychology in the Schools, 38*, 173–184. doi:10.1002/pits.1008

Sznitman, S. R., Reisel, L., & Romer, D. (2011). The neglected role of adolescent emotional well-being in national educational achievement: Bridging the gap between education and mental health policies. *Journal of Adolescent Health, 48*(2), 135–142.

Townsend, B. L. (2000). The disproportionate discipline of African-American learners: Reducing school suspensions and expulsions. *Exceptional Children, 66*, 381–391. doi:10.1177/001440290006600308

Tyack, D., & Cuban, L. (1995). *Tinkering Toward Utopia: A Century of Public School Reform.* Cambridge, MA: Harvard University Press.

Vincent, G. M., Grisso, T., Terry, A., & Banks, S. (2008). Sex and race differences in mental health symptoms in juvenile justice: The MAYSI-2 national meta-analysis. *Journal of the American Academy of Child & Adolescent Psychiatry, 47*(3), 282–290.

Part I

Health behaviors and educational outcomes

1 A dream deferred

How trauma impacts the academic achievement of African American youth

Larry J. Walker and Ramon B. Goings

Throughout the 20th century public schools experienced considerable political and social change, including the influx of immigrants from Eastern and Western Europe, the rise of teacher unions, and successful court challenges including *Brown v Board of Education*. Collectively these events dramatically altered the ethnic and racial composition of the American public school system. Schools became the flashpoint for a nation struggling to find its identity post Reconstruction. The *Brown* court case represented a watershed moment in U.S. history. After the ruling, African Americans believed the vestiges of slavery were being slowly wiped away to create a fair and balanced system. For instance, school districts would have to end *de jure* practices, which included forcing African American students to attend schools with antiquated facilities and used textbooks. Today public schools located in predominately African American low socioeconomic (SES) communities face similar challenges (Noguera, 2003). In comparison to White students, African American students are more likely to live in communities with disparities due to higher unemployment, incarceration rates, and violence (Walker, 2015). Each factor has a significant impact on student outcomes, including academic achievement.

African American students are exposed to environmental stressors including trauma, which impedes their ability to meet academic benchmarks and develop secure relationships (Cooley-Strickland et al., 2009). Ensuring schools located in low SES communities have the resources to combat these environmental stressors is paramount. Students may experience a variety of primary and secondary traumas including physical danger, feeling threatened, and witnessing or retelling of events (Howard, Budge, & McKay, 2010). Trauma has a short- and long-term impact on human growth and development, familial and peer relationships, and student performance (Bücker et al., 2012). Researchers (Milam, Furr-Holden, & Leaf, 2010) examined the relationship between community safety, violence, and academic achievement for urban youth (3rd–8th graders) and found a correlation between community stressors and reading and math scores.

According to the American Psychiatric Association (2000), trauma is a "direct personal experience of an event that involves actual or threatened death or serious injury, or other threat to one's physical integrity; or witnessing an event that involves death" (p. 463). Trauma impacts cognition, which influences a student's ability to retain and analyze information. Overstreet and Mathews (2011) assert that "exposure to specific types of trauma has been linked to an array of negative mental health and academic outcomes" (p. 738). It is important that practitioners understand that trauma is pervasive in communities with limited resources and high rates of violence. Aiding students who struggle to understand complex factors including family, community, and school violence is vital. Without this aid, student behaviors and school performance may suffer.

Providing comprehensive mental health resources to children could mediate trauma's effect on academic achievement (Daigneault, Hébert, & Tourigny, 2007). Without vital support, students do not have the coping skills to function after a singular or continuous traumatic event(s). Far too often, administrators and teachers misinterpret combative behaviors as an overall reflection of a student's ability to learn or interact with peers. Students who exhibit troubling behaviors in the classroom are seeking help. Thus, suggesting they are "bad" or "difficult to teach" will not address core issues including exposure to violence.

Victims of trauma sometimes struggle with anxiety, depression, or post-traumatic stress disorder (PTSD). They may relive experiences, which can negatively impact student outcomes and potentially be responsible for decreased school success (Overstreet & Mathews, 2011). Investigating the interconnected relationship between trauma and academic achievement requires a layered approach. Researchers are developing new theories that contextualize issues unique to minority and underserved communities.

Utilizing critical race theory (CRT), Ladson-Billings and Tate (1995) reframed the education debate by stating the significance of race in determining inequities in the United States. McGee and Stovall (2015) suggest that CRT can help educators and researchers understand how trauma and race impact student outcomes. For these reasons, CRT represents one of two theoretical frameworks guiding this chapter. The second framework is rooted in principles that investigate how environmental factors affect academic achievement (Bronfenbrenner, 1979). Students encounter a variety of experiences that shape their school performance, and peer-to-peer and teacher relationships. Community, familial relationships, and school culture can be significant barriers or advantages for students from underserved backgrounds. Examining interrelated factors can help administrators, advocates, educators, policy makers, and researchers develop policies and programs to meet the diverse needs of African American students. Thus, this chapter explores the relationship between environmental factors and academic achievement for African American students in PreK–5 settings within the levels of Bronfenbrenner's framework.

INDIVIDUAL LEVEL: CHILDHOOD TRAUMA, AND PHYSICAL AND MENTAL HEALTH

Increasingly researchers are connecting traumatic experiences during childhood to adverse chemical and cognitive functioning throughout the lifespan

(Duplechain, Reigner, & Packard, 2008). Students from low SES backgrounds are not thriving and face dangers that significantly impact their ability to succeed. The strain from living in underresourced communities is related to physical and mental health conditions including childhood obesity, anxiety, depression, and PTSD. In addition, students exposed to trauma have to overcome physiological problems that may hamper their ability to thrive and complete simple or complex tasks (Nikulina, Widom, & Czaja, 2011).

Findings from Assari, Lankarani, Caldwell, and Zimmerman (2015) found a relationship between environmental stressors and cortisol levels. The release of cortisol, a hormone, can hinder growth and behavioral functioning. The findings are troubling considering the correlation between race and environmental stressors including trauma (Alim et al., 2006). Far too often, African American students from low SES communities experience intrafamilial and community violence. Short- and long-term exposure to violence can lead to outcomes including PTSD and anxiety. Unfortunately, for undiagnosed students their behaviors sometimes disrupt teachers who may not recognize symptoms associated with PTSD. Students with repeated exposure to trauma may be incapable of regulating their emotions or unable to complete class assignments. Researchers including Finkelhor, Ormond, and Turner (2007) studied children from ages 2 to 17 and determined that more than half of the participants were physically assaulted within the last year. School districts should provide teachers with professional development opportunities to recognize a student in distress (Sinanan, 2011). Without proper training, members of the school-based staff may not recognize the effects of trauma on their students. Students may exhibit dissociative traits to overcome a singular or multiple traumas, which manifest as disruptive classroom behaviors. Teachers may assume students cannot remember specific lessons or events because they are not paying attention. Students could appear distracted or struggle to comprehend reading or math lessons. Recognizing signs, including distractibility or loss of memory, could help students in need of counseling.

Early exposure to trauma has a considerable impact on the lives of children, adolescents, and adults. African Americans are among the nation's most vulnerable subgroups because of higher rates of poverty. Tough (2009) contends, "Black Americans are more likely than white Americans to be consistently poor for a long period; when whites experience poverty, it is more likely for a limited time" (p. 99). Countering years of structural racism will require a comprehensive approach that addresses economic, political, and social systems. Individuals with PTSD sometimes struggle to rationalize events and control emotions, including isolation and feeling trapped. Moreover, "the high incidence of socioemotional and behavior problems is consistent with the notion that trauma victims, especially those who endure chronic victimization, suffer overwhelming amounts of stress" (Overstreet & Mathews, 2011, p. 741).

INTERRELATIONAL LEVEL: FAMILIAL, COMMUNITY RELATIONSHIPS, AND SCHOOL CULTURE

Familial bonds play an important role in the lives of African Americans. Families serve as children's first teachers shaping the overall perspective of impressionable students eager to develop secure relationships with caring adults. Throughout development, relationships with immediate, extended family, and the community influence their social emotional health and academic achievement. Negative interactions with family, peers, and community members may contribute to anxiety, depression, and destructive behaviors. Ensuring students exposed to external stressors including trauma have access to therapeutic services is important. In these cases, providing emotional scaffolding can help students to overcome environmental factors.

African American students from underserved communities are more likely to encounter violence in comparison to White students (Pole, Gone, & Kulkarni, 2008). Increased exposure to violence by elementary school–aged students is linked to a variety of long-term problems including substance abuse, self-destructive behaviors, and dropping out of school (Porsche, Fortuna, Lin, & Alegria, 2011). Consistent exposure to violence contributes to low school performance, increased dropout rates, and long-term mental health problems (Voisin, Neilands, & Hunnicutt, 2011). Although schools play an important role in shielding students from neighborhood conflicts, schools may also place students at risk. Some students are victims of bullying, defined as physical harassment, threats, electronic intimidation, and verbal threats (Litwiller & Brausch, 2013), which increases absenteeism rates (Roman & Taylor, 2013).

There is an important link between school culture, bullying, and victimization among African American students. Schools in neighborhoods with limited resources and high levels of community violence need to provide safe spaces, as the communities themselves may not be able to offer safe alternatives for students. Providing these additional resources would not only shield students but also lead to improved student outcomes. Schools that are perceived as unsafe, on the other hand, can increase the risk of bullying and victimization (Patton, Hong, Williams, & Allen-Meares, 2013). Students who are victims or witnesses of intrafamilial violence struggle to reconcile events at home with nurturing school environments. Unfortunately, students forced to cope with traumatic experiences at home exhibit defiant behaviors at school that contribute to low academic performance and increased suspension rates. Continuous or sporadic exposure to violence hinders a student's ability to concentrate, work collaboratively with classmates, and develop strong social skills. Families are a critical link that anchors students during turbulent times; but without a strong connection between caregivers and students, students sail adrift like ships in a stormy sea. Consequently, preventing students from failing is predicated on the efforts of members of the school-based staff. Identifying students in need of intervention strategies could improve school performance and relationships with peers and teachers.

SCHOOL/COMMUNITY LEVEL: ADDRESSING MALADAPTIVE BEHAVIORS

Developing secure relationships with students and parents can improve student academic achievement and open the lines of communication (Boykin & Noguera, 2011). Creating a sense of trust is vital for communities gripped by intergenerational poverty. Tearing down barriers requires an empathetic approach, which includes working collaboratively with stakeholders to address systemic issues. Unfortunately, students from predominantly African American, underserved communities encounter a plethora of barriers because of uneven housing policies and archaic school finance laws (Hochschild, Scovronick, & Scovronick, 2004). Living in neighborhoods with limited resources and government investment contributes to economic conditions that preserve historical inequities.

For students in PreK–5 settings, trauma is frequently a precursor to combative behaviors that disrupt learning. Outcomes can include decreased reading scores and an increase in aggressive interactions with peers and teachers (Duplechain et al., 2008). Without access to comprehensive services, students may yell, scream, have tantrums, and engage in self-injurious behaviors. Providing training for the school-based staff and committing resources to recruit and retain mental health practitioners is important. School districts are accountable for improving student outcomes including test scores, but this is difficult without additional funding for trained mental health specialists. However, the United States has failed to properly equalize funding between underserved and affluent school districts. Darling-Hammond (2010) stated that "the United States not only has the highest poverty rates for children among industrialized nations, but it also provides fewer social supports for their well-being and few resources for them at school" (p. 31).

Identifying students struggling to overcome traumatic events early is critical to their socioemotional development and academic achievement. Students with maladaptive behaviors in elementary school are likely to continue the same behaviors in middle and high school. According to Basch (2011), "cumulative exposure to aggression and violence, from early childhood to adolescence and adulthood, adversely affects youth in every segment of American society, but consequences are especially harmful for urban minority youth" (p. 619). In spite of limited resources, schools have to devise plans that meet the needs of African American students. This should include seeking partnerships with external groups including foundations and nonprofit organizations to fund innovative programs. Addressing systemic issues is critical considering the problems African American students with limited resources encounter.

Balancing state and federal requirements with the academic and social needs of at-risk youth is complicated. Schools have to meet academic benchmarks but do not have the resources to provide counseling services for traumatized students. Although schools are not equipped to change economic conditions, they can develop proactive approaches to help students. This can be done when there are school leaders cognizant of the barriers that impede student learning. Transformational leaders have the ability to turn around failing schools with limited resources (Collins, 2001). The recruitment and retention of these visionaries can reshape school environments leading to African American student success.

IMPLICATIONS/RECOMMENDATIONS

To support African American youth in PreK–5 settings adults have to make a concerted effort to address systemic inequalities. Our recommendations focus on maintaining systems that support African American youth who experience traumatic events. Specifically, we recommend increasing the availability of school-based practitioners, mental health initiatives, and professional development opportunities for educators.

In recent years several large urban school districts had to cut staff and programs. Consequently, school-based mental health practitioners (psychologists, social workers, counselors) have been eliminated or assigned two to four different schools to provide services to the students. Cutting mental health support negatively impacts student success because students who experience traumatic and/or stressful events do not have access to treatment and support. Moreover, with a potential caseload of 500 or more students, it is impossible for school-based mental health practitioners to adequately support students' needs. This can contribute to employee burnout and negatively impact workforce diversity. For this reason, we recommend an increase in programs designed to support mental health practitioners assigned to schools in pervasively violent communities.

It is important that institutions are responsive to needs of students. In order to support students in PreK–5 settings, schools should provide age-appropriate antibullying lessons and programs. Given the prevalence of cyberbullying, lessons should include discussions of appropriate Internet use including interacting with classmates. In addition, schools should begin outreach efforts for parents so they can identify signs that their child might be in need of mental health services. Proactive outreach efforts can help to destigmatize mental health treatment in the African American community.

School districts have to ensure educators have access to professional development opportunities so they can identify students who may need a mental health evaluation. Using toolkits such as that from Jaycox, Morse, Tanielian, and Stein (2006), which provide exemplars for schools looking to support students who have experienced traumatic events, school districts can develop strategic partnerships with various community mental health organizations and provide educators with tailored professional development.

CONCLUSION

Ensuring schools can support African American students from communities with high rates of community violence exposure is critical. Policy makers have to increase funding so schools can provide mental health services for African American students. This is important considering African American children encounter barriers including low SES, health and lifestyle disparities, and are more likely to attend failing schools in comparison to White students (Darling-Hammond, 2010). Eliminating the resource gap will require significant systemic changes including ending the school to prison pipeline, increasing the number of highly qualified teachers, job creation, and hiring additional counselors and/or psychologists (Boykin & Noguera, 2011).

REFERENCES

Alim, T. N., Graves, E., Mellman, T. A., Aigbogun, N., Gray, E., Lawson, W., & Charney, D. S. (2006). Trauma exposure, posttraumatic stress disorder and depression in an African American primary care population. *Journal of the National Medical Association, 98*(10), 1630.

American Psychiatric Association. (2000). *Diagnostic and statistical manual of mental disorders* (4th ed.). Arlington, VA: American Psychiatric Association.

Assari, S., Lankarani, M. M., Caldwell, C. H., & Zimmerman, M. (2015). Anxiety symptoms during adolescence predicts salivary cortisol in early adulthood among Blacks; sex differences. *International Journal of Endocrinology and Metabolism, 13*(4).

Basch, C. E. (2011). Aggression and violence and the achievement gap among urban minority youth. *Journal of School Health, 81*(10), 619–625.

Boykin, A. W., & Noguera, P. (2011). *Creating the opportunity to learn: Moving from research to practice to close the achievement gap.* Alexandria, VA: ASCD.

Bronfenbrenner, U. (1979). Contexts of child rearing: Problems and prospects. *American Psychologist, 34*(10), 844.

Bücker, J., Kapczinski, F., Post, R., Ceresér, K. M., Szobot, C., Yatham, L. N., & Kauer-Sant'Anna, M. (2012). Cognitive impairment in school-aged children with early trauma. *Comprehensive Psychiatry, 53*(6), 758–764.

Collins, J. C. (2001). *Good to great: Why some companies make the leap... and others don't.* New York: Random House.

Cooley-Strickland, M., Quille, T. J., Griffin, R. S., Stuart, E. A., Bradshaw, C. P., & Furr-Holden, D. (2009). Community violence and youth: Affect, behavior, substance use, and academics. *Clinical Child and Family Psychology Review, 12*(2), 127–156.

Daigneault, I., Hébert, M., & Tourigny, M. (2007). Personal and interpersonal characteristics related to resilient developmental pathways of sexually abused adolescents. *Child and Adolescent Psychiatric Clinics of North America, 16*(2), 415–434.

Darling-Hammond, L. (2010). *The flat world and education: How America's commitment to equity will determine our future.* New York: Teachers College Press.

Duplechain, R., Reigner, R., & Packard, A. (2008). Striking differences: The impact of moderate and high trauma on reading achievement. *Reading Psychology, 29*(2), 117–136.

Finkelhor, D., Ormond, R. K., & Turner, H. A. (2007). Re-victimization patterns in a national longitudinal sample of children and youth. *Child Abuse & Neglect, 31*(5), 479–502.

Hochschild, J. L., Scovronick, N., & Scovronick, N. B. (2004). *The American dream and the public schools.* Oxford, UK: Oxford University Press.

Howard, K. A., Budge, S. L., & McKay, K. M. (2010). Youth exposed to violence: The role of protective factors. *Journal of Community Psychology, 38*(1), 63–79.

Jaycox, L. H., Morse, L. K., Tanielian, T., & Stein, B. D. (2006). How schools can help students recover from traumatic experiences: A tool kit for supporting long-term recovery. RAND Technical Report. Retrieved from http://www.rand.org/content/dam/rand/pubs/technical_reports/2006/RAND_TR413.pdf

Ladson-Billings, G., & Tate, W., IV. (1995). Toward a critical race theory of education. *The Teachers College Record, 97*(1), 47–68.

Litwiller, B. J., & Brausch, A. M. (2013). Cyber bullying and physical bullying in adolescent suicide: The role of violent behavior and substance use. *Journal of Youth and Adolescence, 42*(5), 675–684.

McGee, E. O., & Stovall, D. (2015). Reimagining critical race theory in education: Mental health, healing, and the pathway to liberatory praxis. *Educational Theory, 65*(5), 491–511.

Milam, A. J., Furr-Holden, C. D. M., & Leaf, P. J. (2010). Perceived school and neighborhood safety, neighborhood violence and academic achievement in urban school children. *The Urban Review, 42*(5), 458–467.

Nikulina, V., Widom, C. S., & Czaja, S. (2011). The role of childhood neglect and childhood poverty in predicting mental health, academic achievement and crime in adulthood. *American Journal of Community Psychology, 48*(3–4), 309–321.

Noguera, P. (2003). *City schools and the American dream: Reclaiming the promise of public education.* New York: Teachers College Press.

Overstreet, S., & Mathews, T. (2011). Challenges associated with exposure to chronic trauma: Using a public health framework to foster resilient outcomes among youth. *Psychology in the Schools, 48*(7), 738–754.

Patton, D. U., Hong, J. S., Williams, A. B., & Allen-Meares, P. (2013). A review of research on school bullying among African American youth: An ecological systems analysis. *Educational Psychology Review, 25*(2), 245–260.

Pole, N., Gone, J. P., & Kulkarni, M. (2008). Posttraumatic stress disorder among ethnoracial minorities in the United States. *Clinical Psychology: Science and Practice, 15*(1), 35–61.

Porsche, M. V., Fortuna, L. R., Lin, J., & Alegria, M. (2011). Childhood trauma and psychiatric disorders as correlates of school dropout in a national sample of young adults. *Child Development, 82*(3), 982–998.

Roman, C. G., & Taylor, C. J. (2013). A multilevel assessment of school climate, bullying victimization, and physical activity. *Journal of School Health, 83*(6), 400–407.

Sinanan, A. N. (2011). Bridging the gap of teacher education about child abuse. *Educational Foundations, 25*, 59–73.

Tough, P. (2009). *Whatever it takes: Geoffrey Canada's quest to change Harlem and America.* Boston, MA: Houghton Mifflin Harcourt.

Voisin, D. R., Neilands, T. B., & Hunnicutt, S. (2011). Mechanisms linking violence exposure and school engagement among African American adolescents: Examining the roles of psychological problem behaviors and gender. *American Journal of Orthopsychiatry, 81*(1), 61–71.

Walker, L. (2015). *Trauma, environmental stressors, and the African-American college Student: Research, practice, and HBCUs.* Philadelphia, PA: Penn Center for Minority Serving Institutions. Retrieved from http://www2.gse.upenn.edu/cmsi /content/reports

2 Racism as a fundamental determinant of health for Black boys

Roland J. Thorpe Jr., Derek M. Griffith, Marino A. Bruce, and Lawrence Brown

A fundamental determinant of health is a factor that influences multiple risk factors and multiple disease outcomes and cannot be eliminated simply by addressing the mechanisms that appear to link them to a specific disease (Link & Phelan, 1995). Characterizing racism as a fundamental determinant of health highlights the political, social, and economic environments that influence access to resources necessary to prevent, manage, or overcome disease (Griffith & Johnson, 2013; Griffith, Johnson, Ellis, & Schulz, 2010; Williams & Mohammed, 2013). Fundamental determinants influence health directly through their shaping of environmental and institutional conditions and practices (Krieger, 2008) and through intermediate and proximate factors that impact health outcomes (Schulz, Williams, Israel, & Lempert, 2002).

Fundamental determinants of health, such as racism, are seemingly intractable historical factors that persist over time and lead to disparate health outcomes (Chavez et al., 2004; Griffith, Neighbors, & Johnson, 2009; Schulz & Northridge, 2004). These aspects of the social, political, economic, and cultural environment institutionalize inequality and produce unequally distributed material and social resources. Racism is not a series of isolated incidents or acts, but a deeply ingrained aspect of American life (Grant-Thomas & Powell, 2006; Ladson-Billings & Tate, 1995). Racism is both a process and an outcome that is embedded within the institutional and legal structures of U.S. society (Griffith, Childs, Eng, & Jeffries, 2007; Watts, Griffith, & Abdul-Adil, 1999). Viewed as a process, racism is "an organized system, rooted in an ideology of inferiority that is linked to the political power to categorize, rank, and differentially allocate societal resources to human population groups" (Williams & Rucker, 2000, p. 76). As such, racism influences opportunity structure over the life course by shaping access to environmental resources and stressors critical to African Americans' educational attainment, education outcomes, *and* health behavior and health outcomes.

Racism is not a function of aberrant beliefs or behavior, but it is consistent with U.S. cultural values and tangibly advantages some population groups (Grant-Thomas & Powell, 2006; Ladson-Billings & Tate, 1995). Through the interplay between educational, criminal justice, housing, health, and economic institutions, racism influences health (Grant-Thomas & Powell, 2006).

Social structures, historical legacies, individuals, organizations, and institutions interact to disadvantage some racial groups and advantage others (Jones, 1997).

RACE-BASED NEIGHBORHOOD POLICIES

Race-based residential segregation is pervasive in the United States, structuring access to social and physical resources differentially by racial group (Massey & Denton 1993; Schulz et al., 2002; Williams & Collins, 2001). Though African Americans express higher support for residence in integrated neighborhoods than members of other racial/ethnic groups, race-based residential segregation for African Americans remains high and distinctive (Massey & Denton 1993; Williams & Collins, 2001).

The origins of race-based residential segregation in the United States can be traced back to efforts by White Americans to remain residentially separate from African Americans because of ideological beliefs about the inferiority of African Americans (Collins, 1999). Though the hallmark of segregation as a social policy was separation, from 1896 to 1964 Jim Crow segregation was not just the physical separation of residences by race, but a political ideology based on racism (Bell, 2004). The goal of segregation was to economically, politically, and socially subordinate African Americans to White Americans (Bell, 2004).

Segregation is a manifestation of racism that was legislated by federal, state, and local policies, and supported by economic, cultural (e.g., faith-based organizations), and judicial systems and institutions (Massey & Denton 1993; Williams & Collins, 2001). These policies were reinforced by a variety of local efforts, including housing discrimination and violence by vigilante groups (e.g., the Ku Klux Klan). In addition, allotments of money for educational facilities, infrastructure development, and economic opportunities consistently favored White Americans (Bell, 2004; Williams & Collins, 2004). Thus, it is the unequal distribution of economic, educational, and social resources and opportunities by race, not the racial distribution per se, that results in racial differences in exposure to unequal physical environments, educational systems, and economic opportunities and therefore racial disparities in health (Geronimus & Thompson, 2004; Williams & Collins, 2004).

For African Americans, race-based residential segregation increases social isolation and limits social and economic capital and social mobility (Collins & Williams, 1999; Massey, 2004). Race-based residential segregation leads to poorer real estate investment return and unequal access to community resources through divestment of economic resources and reduction of services. This has important implications for African Americans' ability to accumulate resources and transfer wealth to children and grandchildren (Collins & Williams, 1999). Opportunities for employment are more limited in poverty-dense neighborhoods, and the jobs that are available tend to be either low paying and with few benefits, or high-skill white-collar jobs; however, due

Table 2.1 Segregation and serial forced displacement policies and practices
in the United States

Segregation policies and practices	Displacement policies and practices
Racial zoning	Slum clearance
Racially restrictive covenants	Urban renewal
Redlining	Highway construction and destruction
Public housing site selection	Expulsive zoning via toxic facilities
Public housing resident location	Gentrification
Housing market discrimination	Eminent domain
Little enforcement of 1968 Fair Housing Act	Dismantling of public housing
Little enforcement of 1977 Community Reinvestment Act to undo/stop redlining	Subprime lending by banks leading to mass foreclosures

to compromised educational opportunities, many residents of poverty-dense communities are unable to compete for the white-collar positions (Darden, 1986; Farley, Danziger & Holzer, 2000). Each of these aspects of race-based residential segregation has important implications for educational attainment, health behaviors, and education and health outcomes.

Historically, racism has played a powerful role in shaping both the physical and social environments of Black[1] boys through policies and practices that shape the environments in which they live. Two major types of racist policies and practices affect the life chances and educational outcomes of Black male babies and boys before they enter school around the age of 5: segregation and serial forced displacement (Fullilove & Wallace, 2011; Massey & Tannen, 2015). These policies and practices are listed in Table 2.1.

The policies and practices of segregation and serial forced displacement create disinvested, redlined African American neighborhoods, dilapidated residential housing conditions, and social disorder and disintegration—particularly in urban areas. Massey and Tannen (2015) state that 26% of African Americans in the United States in 2010 lived in hypersegregated cities and of all African Americans living in urban areas, 32% were in cities that are hypersegregated, 21% were in cities that are highly segregated, and 46.1% were in cities that are moderately segregated. Therefore, 53% of African Americans living in urban areas live in a highly or hypersegregated metropolitan area and 99.1% of African Americans living in urban areas live in a city that is at least moderately segregated.

LaVeist, Pollack, Thorpe, Fesahazion, and Gaskin (2011) described the damage that segregation causes African American populations in America by writing: "Racial segregation creates different exposures to economic opportunity and to other community resources that enhance health. Likewise,

---

1 Although the preferred term throughout this book is *African American*, the term *Black* is used often in this chapter, specifically in reference to Black boys or male youth.

segregation produces differential exposure to health risks." Thus, living in a segregated neighborhood is a fundamental driver in producing poorer health for Black boys compared to their counterparts before they begin attending school.

Residential segregation results in inferior funding for schools in the neighborhoods where many Black boys live. In one hypersegregated city—Detroit, Michigan—teachers in the 2015–2016 academic year led a "sick out" to highlight the unhealthy and unsafe conditions of public schools where a disproportionate amount of Black students attend (Higgins, 2016). Dilapidated schools themselves can make Black students sick. Segregation also contributes to the existence of "apartheid schools," which are defined as "schools whose white population is 1 percent or less" (Hannah-Jones, 2014). The more a city is segregated or hypersegregated, the more often Black boys will be attending apartheid schools, which are even less likely to have top-shelf resources and societal support. Additionally, many schools across the South have been released from court-ordered desegregation mandates by judges across the South since 2000 (Hannah-Jones, 2014). This collective judicial rollback of the seminal Supreme Court 1954 decision (*Brown v. Board of Education*) contributes to rising rates of schools that can be classified as apartheid schools in the country.

Two of the top 8 hypersegregated metropolitan areas in America—Flint, Michigan, and Baltimore, Maryland—are in the midst of public health crises revolving around lead poisoning. Both cities are over 60% African American in population. In Flint, hundreds if not thousands of Black babies and boys have been poisoned with lead due to politicians connecting the city to a corrosive water source that caused lead pipes to leach into the city's water supply (Felton, 2016). In Baltimore, hundreds of Black babies and boys are being exposed to lead poison every year due to the lack of strong enforcement and remediation of lead in the housing stock found in disinvested, redlined communities (Wheeler & Broadwater, 2015).

Many Black babies and boys face some form of public health crisis that diminishes their intellectual capacity before entering school, whether through disproportionate exposures to toxic environmental pollution and/or the lack of strong public health action that allows health crises to unfold before the damage has already been done. Freddie Gray is one tragic example of how this happens to thousands of Black male babies across America, especially in disinvested neighborhoods in highly segregated or hypersegregated cities (Fletcher, 2015). Being exposed to lead poison and other toxins as babies not only diminishes Black boys' brain development, but it results in decreased emotional inhibition that contributes to higher rates of crime, violence, and mass incarceration.

The physical environment of neighborhoods like Sandtown-Winchester in Baltimore or the Fifth Ward in Houston is often characterized as food deserts with higher levels of liquor store concentrations, poor sanitation, vacant home density, and closer proximity to toxic chemicals and/or waste. Forced displacement can also alter the physical environment of African American communities, whether it is through highways built through many neighbor-hoods in the 1950s–1970s (Connerly, 2002; Fullilove, 2004), the demolition of public housing that often results in the sale of land to private develop-ers leading to gentrification (Goetz, 2011), or waterfront development in for-merly postindustrial, hypersegregated cities such as Cincinnati or Pittsburgh (Fullilove, 2004). When forced displacement occurs, remaining or nearby African American community members often have little to no input in terms of how the new urban redevelopment will occur (Connerly, 2002; Gomez, 2013).

The involuntary destruction or demolition of one's physical community can result in what psychiatrist Mindy Fullilove calls "root shock." Fullilove (2004) discussed and defined root shock in the following way:

> Root shock is the traumatic stress reaction to the destruction of all or part of one's emotional ecosystem.... Just as the body has a system to main-tain its internal balance, so, too, the individual has a way to maintain the external balance between himself and the world. This way of moving in the environment maximizes the odds that he will survive predators, find food, maintain shelter from the harsh elements, and live in harmony with family and neighbors.

Many hypersegregated cities have created disinvested, redlined African American communities, and have turned to urban redevelopment or gentri-fication policies and practices that will uproot and affect many Black male babies and boys. Redevelopment and gentrification induce root shock for affected African American families. Altering the physical environment of neighborhoods without the empowered participation of residents negatively affects the health of African American families (Gomez, 2013). Due to serial forced displacement, a significant number of Black male babies and boys are forced to navigate new neighborhoods and economic terrains that may be unfamiliar to their parents.

In these ways we describe, racism—vis-à-vis the policies and practices of segregation and serial forced displacement—shapes and impacts the physical environment of Black babies and boys. This damage of racist policies and practices also extends to their social environments. Many Black male babies are born into environments where their fathers are likely to experience high rates of unemployment (Simms, McDaniel, & Monson, 2013), as high as 50% in many urban areas across the country, often due to job sprawl (Stoll, 2005) and transportation policy (Rabin, 1973). Many Black male babies are born into environments where their fathers may no longer be alive due to higher levels of intracommunal homicides or may be incarcerated due to discrimi-natory policing that takes places in disinvested, redlined African American communities.

Discriminatory policing and criminal justice interactions may derive from racial profiling, unequal sentencing laws (i.e., for crack versus pow-der cocaine), or disproportionate arrests due to possession of drugs such as marijuana. Legal scholar Michelle Alexander (2010) calls the aggregation of these interactions the "New Jim Crow." Many Black male babies, especially those born in disinvested, redlined African American communities, are likely to be confronted with the "school-to-prison pipeline" that is a part and parcel of the New Jim Crow. This is especially true since, as Goff, Jackson, Di Leone, Culotta, and DiTomasso (2014) demonstrate, White authority figures overestimate the ages of Black boys, robbing them of their innocence.

Black boys are born into a social environment where they will be subject to greater risk of violence both from other Black males and from police officers. Internal community violence resulting in homicides and police brutality resulting in death are public health threats to Black boys. Black boys are disproportionately exposed to death, violence, and traumatic loss due to homicide at very early ages, often before attending school at the age of 4 or 5 (Smith, 2015). In many urban areas, the vast majority of homicide victims are Black males, therefore young Black boys may experience the traumatic loss due to homicide of another Black male in their social circle by the time they enter school. In terms of the socialization of Black boys, Danielle Wallace (2007) argued that many Black boys are reared in ways that reflect the tremendous psychological stresses that racism imposes on African American parents raising sons, such as the perceived threat of Black masculinity in a White hegemonic society. She suggested due to maladaptive socialization practices, African American parents should begin reevaluating and redefining the definitions of masculinity for Black boys.

Although Massey and Tannen (2015) argued that the number of cities that are hypersegregated is decreasing, their analysis does not account for the levels of occurrence of high levels of the forced displacement of African American populations since 1990—whether in the form of HOPE VI, which resulted in 250,000 demolished public housing units (Goetz, 2013); mass foreclosures due to subprime lending that disproportionately affected African American homebuyers (Lipsitz, 2011; Rugh, Abright, & Massey, 2015); or gentrification in many urban areas (Fullilove & Wallace, 2011; Wharton, 2008). Much of the progress toward desegregation has been achieved by force as opposed to choice. Serial forced displacement undermines the ability of displaced people to wield social capital to help them build sustainable and healthy communities (Fullilove, 2004; Gomez & Muntaner, 2005). As Fullilove and Wallace (2011) have described, mass criminalization leads to mass incarceration, which has resulted in a disproportionate amount of African American fathers and mothers being placed behind bars—constituting another form of root shock resulting in broken families and broken communities.

Another form of forced displacement includes school closures. This is especially an issue in hypersegregated cities since there have been a staggering 464 school closures in the top 8 hypersegregated cities alone since 2000, according to the Journey for Justice Alliance (2014). School closures often mean the loss of a key community resource in these communities for African American families, sometimes one of the few resources in communities that are already resource poor and restricted from obtaining new investments (Journey for Justice Alliance, 2014). The intensification of neoliberal policies means that many African American families are affected by school closures, the privatization of public education, and the rise of charter schools in urban areas. School closures are disproportionately concentrated in disinvested, redlined communities across America, creating impacts that are still being understood, especially in terms of whether educational outcomes improve for Black youth and boys who must often travel farther and to other resource-poor or apartheid schools to continue their education.

GENDER NORMS AND SOCIALIZATION

Jones (1997) argues that culture is a blueprint for living in a society. In a race-conscious society, cultural racism summarizes the attitudes, values, and beliefs that define races and the importance of race in society. Cultural racism comprises the cumulative effects of a racialized worldview, based on belief in essential, biological racial differences that favor White Americans over others. These effects permeate U.S. culture through institutional structures, ideological beliefs, and personal everyday actions of lay people, medical professionals, and public health practitioners and policymakers, and these effects are passed from generation to generation (Jones, 1997; Smedley & Smedley, 2005). These cultural values and beliefs about race tell people what is appropriate to think, how it is appropriate to act, and what values are important to promote in reference to people of different racial and ethnic groups (Jones, 1997).

Consequently, cultural views about race and cultural racism have profound implications for health by influencing interpersonal interactions and the norms, policies, and practices of organizations, institutions, and society. The cumulative effects of living in a society and culture that hierarchically ranks people of socially defined races (LaVeist, 2002; Smedley & Smedley, 2005) is an important foundation for understanding racism as a determinant of education and health outcomes for African American males. Many African American boys will be subjected to highly racialized beliefs about and portrayals of themselves. Many African American males' experiences with and views about race have social and psychological implications that influence their educational outcomes. Therefore, the concept of race is likely to influence academic aspirations and/or achievement of some African American boys before or by the time they enter school (Rowley & Bowman, 2009).

U.S. cultural notions of racial inferiority and superiority become part of institutional structures and processes that in turn organize and promote the values and standards of a race-conscious society (Jones, 1997). Institutional racism has been defined as a systematic set of patterns, procedures, practices, and policies that operate within institutions so as to consistently penalize, disadvantage, and exploit communities and individuals of color (Better, 2008). The concept describes the systematic operation of an institution and highlights the historical, social, and political aspects of systems that influence practices and policies that may not seem to be affected by race but can still produce differential outcomes (Griffith et al., 2007). Two important aspects of institutional racism are race-based residential segregation and institutional racism in education.

Cultural notions of male gender are similar to cultural racism. Complex and dynamic, gender intersects with cultural racism to influence the cultural schemas that shape African American men's lives and cancer outcomes. Male gender is signified by beliefs and behaviors that are practiced in social inter-actions and, therefore, varies between cultures, subcultures, and individuals (Moynihan, 1998). For African American boys, race, identity, and ideals of masculinity are often defined by White society. Many African American boys are socialized to think of masculinity as the pursuit of symbols of economic standing and sexual opportunity (Hooks, 1992).

African American men's sense of racial and gender identity are shaped by broader processes of cultural socialization: the broader context for under-standing gender, ethnicity, sexual orientation, and racial identity development (Stevenson, 1997). It is not only through interaction with people of their own race, gender, or identity group that is important, but it is how people are treated when they interact with people of other groups, and how that differ-ence is interpreted, that influences how people see themselves and their group membership. For African American men, this process is not one of simply race or gender, but the intersection of the two.

ADDRESSING RACISM'S EFFECTS ON AFRICAN AMERICAN MALES

Given these structural, institutional, and cultural realities, how do we address racism's effects on African American males before they reach our elementary classrooms? Since racism's power to impact and affect Black male babies and boys derives from its structural, institutional, and cultural forces, our solu-tions to address and ameliorate racism's effects must operate simultaneously on these terrains.

Structural remedies to racism will include acknowledging the damage and harm that it has caused the entire African American community as a fun-damental determinant of health as we mentioned at the beginning of this chapter. One way to address this harm is through reparations as scholars such as Gaskin, Headen, and White-Means (2005) or writers such as Coates (2014) have argued. Gaskin and colleagues argue that reparations should be allo-cated in part based on the damage that racism has caused to the health of African American individuals and families. Given the extensive damage that racism has caused and continues to cause, reparations should be a critical component of helping bolster the health of future Black male babies and boys in America.

Aside from reparations, other structural solutions should focus on enforcing existing policies or restoring practices that help address structural inequity such as reinstituting court-enforced desegregation consent decrees in order to reduce the number of apartheid schools that Black boys will attend. Other structural remedies include enforcing the affirmatively furthering mandate found in the 1968 Fair Housing Act (Hannah-Jones, 2014) and anti-redlining provisions found in the 1974 Equal Credit Opportunity Act and the 1977 Community Reinvestment Act (Massey & Tannen, 2015). Strong federal enforcement action must also take place in terms of punishing banks and prosecuting bank officials for discriminatory subprime lending, racial steering, and redlining, which is still occurring around the nation in order to address the structural effects of segregation and serial forced displacement. Some practices must be countered such as turning back efforts to undermine the 1965 Voting Rights Act through voter restriction initiatives currently underway. Many structural efforts should be developed to help assist African American fathers in remaining involved in the lives of their children. For instance, social policies such as the War on Drugs, welfare, and child support often work more to remove African American fathers from the household and keep them from being an active presence in the lives of Black male babies and boys.

Much of the structural work that must take place must directly tackle persisting segregation and ongoing forced displacement. A great deal of the damage that racism causes is through its impact on the places and spaces where African American families live. Given that 53% of African Americans living in urban areas are living in a highly segregated or hypersegregated city, millions of Black male babies and boys are exposed to damaging and unhealthy physical and social environments. Additionally, due to serial forced displacement policies and practices, these babies and boys are likely to be impacted by the far-reaching ripples of root shock as their families experience stress related to forced housing instability, and their neighborhoods are weakened by diminished social capital, school closures, and redevelopment without the input of lower-income African American people. Hence, addressing segregation and serial forced displacement will improve millions of Black male babies' and boys' access to healthy physical and social environments, bolster their families' housing stability, and increase their neighborhoods' levels of social capital and well-resourced community schools.

In terms of the institutional effects of racism, health departments around the nation must begin mobilizing in order to counter the environmental impacts on Black boys and their health. We know that Black boys are confronted with higher levels of lead poisoning than their White counterparts, which affect their learning capacity and ability to regulate their emotions, potentially contributing to higher levels of crime and violence later in their lives. For instance, in Flint, Michigan, and Baltimore, Maryland—which are currently undergoing lead poison and health crises—these cities' health departments should be engaged in swift and effective lead remediation, chelation therapy for lead poisoning victims, asthma education and prevention interventions, providing more comprehensive neonatal resources to pregnant African American mothers to eliminate disparities in low birth weight infants, and linking Black boys who may be suffering from PTSD due to violence or the traumatic loss of homicide to culturally relevant mental health therapy. Local philanthropic institutions, nonprofit agencies, and grassroots organizations must begin to empower communities with funding and control to develop their own interventions to counter racism's health impact. Governmental environmental agencies must also begin to strongly enforce environmental protection laws against corporations that disproportionately release toxic pollutants into African American neighborhoods in which Black male babies and boys live.

Careful work must also ensue to address the cultural effects of racism on the lives and health of Black boys. For instance, more marketing campaigns must be started to counteract the negative perceptions of academic achievement or the stereotypical portrayals that depict Black boys and men as intellectually inferior, academically incapable, or innately athletic (but not academically inclined). These damaging stereotypes are already at work in the media before Black boys enter school, therefore anti-stereotype social marketing campaigns will need to take place in the domain of media to help counteract these pervasive stereotypes.

These stereotypes are most likely to take root in disinvested, redlined African American neighborhoods and families that have been damaged by decades of segregation and serial forced displacement. These segregated environments negatively affect Black male role socialization and young Black boys' developing sense of masculinity and gender identity as discussed earlier. In many ways, changing how Black boys are socialized to negate the impact of racism on the development of masculinity is nigh impossible while Black boys are growing up in highly or hypersegregated cities inside of disinvested neighborhoods filled with dilapidated housing and high unemployment. Culture is developed and practiced in concert with one's environment. Therefore, we recommend parenting empowerment courses for African American families that come connected with real opportunity—whether in terms of housing mobility vouchers to well-resourced communities or investing heavily, rebuilding, and strengthening America's neglected, disinvested, and redlined African American communities without forcing existing populations to relocate as the community begins to improve. With more traditional banks engaging in fair lending to African American homebuyers and small business owners, more African American parents, but fathers especially, will be able to gain sustainable employment or entrepreneurial ownership of businesses in increasingly resourced neighborhoods. This will enable more African American fathers to provide greater levels of economic support for their children and help a greater number of African American fathers coparent their babies and boys. More financial empowerment and entrepreneurial ownership means that more African American families will be covered by health insurance and able to afford better plans that will help them address health issues that may arise for Black male babies and boys in the womb before they reach the classroom.

In short, we recognize that combating racism's manifold effects on the health of African American male babies and boys requires addressing multiple structural, institutional, and cultural factors simultaneously and powerfully. Inasmuch as the damage of racism has been imposed on African American families, the solutions to address the preclassroom health and well-being of African American boys must be applied in an equally vigorous and multi-level fashion to be effective. Addressing racism's health effects on African American boys' ages 0 to 5 will require an intergenerational advocacy effort that involves building institutions and movements that will work to bring about improved health outcomes. With the framework we have provided here and commitment from African American communities, institutions, and families, we can achieve our objective: neutralizing racism's impact on the health and well-being of African American boys from womb to classroom.

REFERENCES

Alexander, M. (2010). *The new Jim Crow: Mass incarceration in the age of colorblind-ness*. New York: New Press.

Bell, D. A. (2004). *Silent covenants: Brown v. Board of Education and the unfulfilled hopes for racial reform*. Oxford, UK: Oxford University Press.

Better, S. (2008). *Institutional racism: A primer on theory and strategies for social change*. Lanham, MD: Rowman & Littlefield.

Chavez, V., Israel, B., Allen, A. J., 3rd, DeCarlo, M. F., Lichtenstein, R., Schulz, A., ... McGranaghan, R. (2004). A Bridge Between Communities: Video-making using principles of community-based participatory research. *Health Promotion Practice, 5*, 4, 395–403. Retrieved from http://www.ncbi.nlm.nih.gov/entrez/query.fcgi?cmd =Retrieve&db=PubMed&dopt=Citation&list_uids=15358912

Coates, T. (2014). The case for reparations. *The Atlantic.* Retrieved from http://www .theatlantic.com/features/archive/2014/05/the-case-for- reparations/361631/

Collins, C. A. (1999). Racism and health: Segregation and causes of death amenable to medical intervention in major U.S. cities. *Annals of the New York Academy of Sciences, 896*, 396–398.

Collins, C. A., & Williams, D. R. (1999). *Segregation and mortality: The deadly effects of racism?* Paper presented at the Sociological Forum.

Connerly, C. E. (2002). From racial zoning to community empowerment: The Interstate Highway System and the African American community in Birmingham, Alabama. *Journal of Planning Education and Research, 22*, 2, 99–114.

Darden, J. T. (1986). The significance of race and class in residential segregation. *Journal of Urban Affairs, 8*, 1, 49–56.

Farley, R., Danziger, S., & Holzer, H. (2000). *Detroit divided*. New York: Russell Sage Foundation.

Felton, R. (2016). Flint's water crisis: What went wrong. *The Guardian.* January 16. Retrieved from http://www.theguardian.com/environment/2016/jan/16/flints-water -crisis-what-went-wrong

Fletcher, M. A. (2015). Freddie Gray and William Porter: Two sons of Baltimore whose lives collided. *The Washington Post*, September 3, p. A1. Retrieved from https://www.washingtonpost.com/local/freddie-gray-and-william-porter-two -sons-of-baltimore-whose-lives-collided/2015/09/03/a6273e5c-4a66-11e5-846d -02792f854297_story.html

Fullilove, M. (2004). *Root shock: How tearing up city neighborhoods hurts America, and what we can do about it*. New York: Ballentine.

Fullilove, M. T., & Wallace, R. (2011). Serial forced displacement in American cities, 1916–2010. *Journal of Urban Health*, 88, 3, 381–389. doi:10.1007/s11524-011-9585-2

Gaskin, D. J., Headen, A. E., & White-Means, S. I. (2005). Racial disparities in health and wealth: The effects of slavery and past discrimination. *The Review of Black Political Economy, 32*, 95–110.

Geronimus, A. T., & Thompson, J. P. (2004). To denigrate, ignore, or disrupt: Racial inequality in health and impact of a policy-induced breakdown of Black American communities. *DuBois Review: Social Science Research on Race, 1*, 2, 247–279.

Goetz, E. (2011). Gentrification in Black and White: The racial impact of public housing demolition in American Cities. *Urban Studies, 48*, 1581–1604. doi: 10.1177/0042098010375323

Goetz, E. G. (2013). *New deal ruins: Race, economic justice, and public housing policy* (1st ed.). Cornell University Press.

Goff, P. A., Jackson, M. C., Di Leone, B. A., Culotta, C. M., & DiTomasso, N. A. (2014). The essence of innocence: Consequences of dehumanizing Black children. *Journal of Personality and Social Psychology, 106*, 4, 526–45.

Gomez, M. B. (2013). *Race, class, power, and organizing in East Baltimore: Rebuilding abandoned communities in America*. Lanham, Maryland: Lexington Books.

Gomez, M. B., & Muntaner, C. (2005). Urban redevelopment and neighborhood health in East Baltimore, Maryland: The role of communitarian and institutional social capital. *Critical Public Health, 15*, 2, 83–102. doi:10.1080/09581590500183817

Grant-Thomas, A., & Powell, J. (2006). Toward a structural racism framework. *Poverty & Race, 15*, 6, 3–6.

Griffith, D. M., Childs, E. L., Eng, E., & Jeffries, V. (2007). Racism in organizations: The case of a county health department. *Journal of Community Psychology, 35*, 3, 291–306. doi: 10.1002/jcop.20149

Griffith, D. M., & Johnson, J. L. (2013). Implications of racism for African American men's cancer risk, morbidity and mortality. In H. M. Treadwell, C. Xanthos, K. B. Holden, & R. L. Braithwaite (Eds.), *Social determinants of health among African American Men* (pp. 21–38). New York: Jossey-Bass.

Griffith, D. M., Johnson, J., Ellis, K. R., & Schulz, A. J. (2010). Cultural context and a critical approach to eliminating health disparities. *Ethnicity and Disease, 20*, 1, 71–76.

Griffith, D. M., Neighbors, H. W., & Johnson, J. (2009). Using national data sets to improve the health of Black Americans: Challenges and opportunities. *Cultural Diversity and Ethnic Minority Psychology, 15*, 1, 86–95.

Hannah-Jones, N. (2014). Segregation now. *The Atlantic*. May. Retrieved from http:// www.theatlantic.com/magazine/archive/2014/05/segregation-now/359813/

Higgins, L. (2016). DPS teachers at rally: Sick-outs a demand to be heard. *Detroit Free Press*. January 15. Detroit. Retrieved from http://www.freep.com/story/news/local /michigan/detroit/2016/01/11/dps-schools-closed-sickouts/78618800/

Hooks, B. (1992). Representations of whiteness in the black imagination *Black looks: Race and representation* (pp. 165–178). London, UK: Turnaround.

Jones, J. M. (1997). *Prejudice and Racism (2nd ed.)*. New York: McGraw-Hill Companies.

Journey for Justice Alliance. (2014). *Death by a thousand cuts: Racism, school closures, and public school sabotage*. Retrieved from http://b.3cdn.net/advancement/3739088 d8cb8488bdf_6jm62a5i6.pdf

Krieger, N. (2008). Proximal, distal, and the politics of causation: What's level got to do with it? *American Journal Public Health*, 98, 2, 221–230.

Ladson-Billings, G., & Tate, W. F. (1995). Toward a critical race theory of education. *Teachers College Record, 97*, 1, 47–68.

LaVeist, T. (2002). Segregation, poverty, and empowerment: Health consequences for African Americans. In T. A. LaVeist (Ed.), *Race, ethnicity, and health: A public health reader* (pp. 76–96). San Francisco, CA: Jossey-Bass.

LaVeist, T., Pollack, K., Thorpe, R. J., Fesahazion, R., & Gaskin, D. (2011). Place, not race: Disparities dissipate in southwest Baltimore when blacks and whites live under similar conditions. *Health Affairs*, 30, 10, 1880–1887.

Link, B. G., & Phelan, J. (1995). Social conditions as fundamental causes of disease. *Journal of Health and Social Behavior, 35* (Extra Issue), 80–94.

Lipsitz, G. (2011). *How racism takes place*. Philadelphia, PA: Temple University Press.

Massey, D. S. (2004). Segregation and stratification: A biosocial perspective. *Du Bois Review: Social Science Research on Race*, 1, 1, 7–25.

Massey, D. S., & Tannen, J. (2015). A research note on trends in Black hypersegregation. *Demography*, *52*, 3, 1025–1043. doi:10.1007/s13524-015-0381-6

Massey, D. S., & Denton, N. A. (1993). *American apartheid: Segregation and the making of the underclass*. Cambridge, Mass: Harvard University Press.

Moynihan, C. (1998). Theories in health care and research: Theories of masculinity. *British Medical Journal, 317*, 1072–1075.

Rabin, Y. (1973). Highways as a barrier to equal access. *The Annals of the American Academy of Political and Social Science, 407*, 63–77.

Rowley, L. L., & Bowman, P. J. (2009). Risk, protection, and achievement disparities among African American males: Cross-generation theory, research, and comprehensive intervention. *The Journal of Negro Education*, 305–320.

Rugh, J. S., Albright, L., & Massey, D. S. (2015). Race, space, and cumulative disadvantage: A case study of the subprime lending collapse. *Social Problems, 62*, 186–218. doi:10.1093/socpro/spv002

Schulz, A., & Northridge, M. E. (2004). Social determinants of health: Implications for environmental health promotion. *Health, Education, & Behavior, 31*, 4, 455–471. Retrieved from http://www.ncbi.nlm.nih.gov/entrez/query.fcgi?cmd=Retrieve &db=PubMed&dopt=Citation&list_uids=15296629

Schulz, A. J., Williams, D. R., Israel, B. A., & Lempert, L. B. (2002). Racial and spatial relations as fundamental determinants of health in Detroit. *Milbank Quarterly, 80*, 4, 677–707, iv. Retrieved from http://www.ncbi.nlm.nih.gov/entrez/query.fcgi?cmd =Retrieve&db=PubMed&dopt=Citation&list_uids=12532644

Simms, M., McDaniel, M., & Monson, W. (2013). *Low-income men at the margins caught at the intersection of race, place, and poverty*. Retrieved from http://www .urban.org/publications/412987.html

Smedley, A., & Smedley, B. D. (2005). Race as biology is fiction, racism as a social problem is real: Anthropological and historical perspectives on the social construction of race. *American Psychologist, 60*, 1, 16–26. doi: 2005-00117-003

Stevenson, H. C. (1997). Managing anger: Protective, proactive or adaptive racial socialization identity profiles and African-American manhood development. In R. J. Watts & R. J. Jagers (Eds), *Manhood Development in Urban African-American Communities* (pp. 35–61). Portland, OR: Hawthorne Press.

Smith, J. R. (2015). Unequal burdens of loss: Examining the frequency and timing of homicide deaths experienced by young Black men across the life course. *American Journal of Public Health*, e1–e8. doi:10.2105/AJPH.2014.302535

Stoll, M. A. (2005). *Job sprawl and the spatial mismatch between Blacks and jobs.* Washington, DC: Brookings Institution.

Wallace, D. (2007). "It's a M-A-N Thang": Black male gender role socialization and the performance of masculinity in love relationships. *The Journal of Pan African Studies, 1*, 7, 11–22.

Watts, R. J., Griffith, D. M., & Abdul-Adil, J. (1999). Sociopolitical development as an antidote for oppression. *American Journal of Community Psychology, 27*, 2, 255–271.

Wharton, J. L. (2008). Gentrification: The new colonialism in the modern era. *Forum on Public Policy: A Journal of the Oxford Round Table*. Summer.

Wheeler, T., & Broadwater, L. (2015). Lead paint: Despite progress, hundreds of Maryland children still poisoned. *Baltimore Sun*, December 5, p. A1.

Williams, D. R., & Collins, C. (2001). Racial residential segregation: A fundamental cause of racial disparities in health. *Public Health Reports, 116*, 5, 404–416.

Williams, D. R., & Collins, C. (2004). Reparations: A viable strategy to address the enigma of African American health. *American Behavioral Scientist, 47*, 7, 977–1000.

Williams, D. R., & Mohammed, S. A. (2013). Racism and health I: Pathways and scientific evidence. *American Behavioral Scientist, 57*, 8, 1152–1173. doi:10.1177/0002764213487340

Williams, D. R., & Rucker, T. D. (2000). Understanding and addressing racial disparities in health care. *Health Care Financing Review, 21*, 4, 75–90.

3 Drinking and learning while Black

The effect of family problem drinking on children's later educational attainment

Stacey Houston II

Researchers have long been interested in the ways that people and groups of people respond to various stressors. One of the groups most often studied is the family, as the family is arguably the most basic social unit of our society. Within the framework of family stress theory, scholars have uncovered a number of stressors (e.g., perceived neighborhood disorder, marital disruption, and economic hardship) that lead to an array of outcomes (Anderson, 2002; Elder, Liker, & Cross, 1984; Elder, Nguyen, & Capsi, 1985; Kotchick, Dorsey, & Heller, 2005; Mannino & Deutsch, 2007; McCubbin & Patterson, 1982; Wang & Amato, 2000). Oftentimes the outcome of interest involves the children of the family, one of the most protected populations in our society. The logic of family stress theory is that stressors are present in all families. In turn, families and the individuals in them have resources that help them deal with these stressors. Based on the stressor and the resources available, families and family members adapt in response to that stressor in order to try to maintain equilibrium in the family. The adaptation that occurs often results in negative outcomes for children, such as diminished psychological functioning, reduced health, and/or poorer academic performance. Thus, the presence of stressors in families results in children being labeled "at risk" (Nicolas et al., 2008).

In line with family stress theory, resilience theory provides the opportunity to replace the negative outcomes of stressors, risks, or adversity with positive outcomes. Resilience, the ability to bounce back, has recently surfaced as a critical piece of the stress theory puzzle. Contrary to early understandings, stressors do not function similarly for all groups of people, and scholars have found marked differences in response to stressors by both gender and race (Borman & Overman, 2004; Hollister-Wagner, Foshee, & Jackson, 2001). Similar to family stress theory, resilience theory suggests that individuals are embedded in networks that provide resources to effectively cope with the presence of stressors. Resilience theory, thus, provides the opportunity for researchers to theorize differential outcomes that result from stressors in the family.

Despite the fact that resilience theory suggests some people tend to bounce back in the face of adversity, family stress theory should not be dismissed.

Researchers who ground their studies with family stress theory have been correct to assume that all families experience some perceivably stressful event and the concomitant adaptation results in some outcome for the family unit and individuals in the family. However, universality and generalizability of what constitutes stressors remains questionable. The purpose of this chapter is to revisit family stress theory using a family history of problem drinking as the stressor and educational attainment of children as the outcome measure, and also to revisit resilience theory to examine whether a family history of problem drinking is a universal stressor across race. The main research questions are: Is there a relationship between having a family history of problem drinking and educational attainment? And, does race moderate the effects of having a family history of problem drinking on educational attainment?

By uncovering how this stressor functions differently for White Americans and African Americans, results from this chapter call into question the detrimental effects of stressors that often show up in large samples that have not been disaggregated. In doing so, the chapter concurrently raises questions regarding the labeling of certain groups of youths as "at risk." Though not concluding that certain groups of children should, indeed, face adversity, this chapter does suggests that there may be characteristics of African American youth, namely their families, that could be capitalized upon to help foster resiliency and thereby decrease the dreaded achievement gap.

ALCOHOLISM IN CONTEXT: FAMILY STRESS THEORY

According to the family stress model, exposure to stressful life events increases psychological distress, which creates, or exacerbates, behavioral and emotional maladjustment (Kotchick et al., 2005). Oftentimes, family stress theory is linked to stressors that impair parenting, called parental psychological distress, which then open the door to abnormal child behavioral and emotional development. More generally, however, family stress theory assumes that all families are subjected to some stressor. Empirical support of this theory has taken a variety of forms but has its roots in studies conducted by Elder and his colleagues who examined the effect of the Great Depression as a stressor on various facets of family functioning (Elder et al., 1984, 1985). This research, which has been replicated in more contemporary studies, linked economic hardship with fathers' psychological distress and disruptions in parenting (Conger et al., 1992; Conger, Ge, Elder, Lorenz, & Simon, 1994; McLoyd, Jayaratne, Ceballo, & Borquez, 1994).

Though economic hardship is at the root of family stress theory, it has since grown to encompass other stressors such as marital disruption, intimate partner violence, household division of labor, and perceived neighborhood disorder (Anderson, 2002; Kotchick et al., 2005; Mannino & Deutsch, 2007; Wang & Amato, 2000). One phenomenon that has not received much attention via a family stress lens is alcoholism. According to family stress theory, the stressors that families face as a result of the presence of an alcoholic family member likely result in increased psychological distress in parents and children. Though this chapter does not deal directly with clinically diagnosed alcoholism, the assumption is that problem drinking is a pre-alcoholism condition that similarly affects families and individuals. Research that does exist on alcoholism demonstrates that chronic overconsumption of alcohol is associated with psychological and physical impairment (McCord, 1972; Nardi, 1981). For example, one psychological study on 54 children conducted by Reich, Earls, and Powell (2006) demonstrates that this psychological impairment leads to diminished functioning of the family, characterized by marital conflict, parent–child conflict, and, in some cases, child physical abuse.

Generally, whether researchers who utilize family stress theory focus on economic hardship or family structure disruption, they tend to conclude that the adaptation that a family makes in the face of the stressor results in detrimental outcomes. Previous research, however, has shown that some groups of people experience a buffer to stress. For example, previous research has shown that many African American single mothers do not engage in negative parenting behaviors despite the financial challenges and community-related risks they face (Murry, Bynum, Brody, Willert, & Stephens, 2001). Other research has concluded that social support serves as a buffer to the otherwise negative effect of stressors (Belsky, 1984). In the case of African American mothers, informal social support from family and friends serves as a protective factor as they often rely on their extended family and friend networks for support in childbearing tasks and parenting duties. Important for this study, African American children who have parents and grandparents that drink heavily may likely benefit from the social support of other nonalcoholic family members and friends and, thus, not be affected by the psychological distress that arises from the presence of problem drinking.

While family stress theory provides room for these buffers that allow families to return to equilibrium, less work has been done that explains how families and family members experience growth or positive effects in the face of perceived stressors. Furthermore, family stress theory accounts for buffers, which prevent stressors from altering the equilibrium of family functioning. However, questions remain regarding instances in which events that have been universally labeled as stressors might result in effects in the opposite direction from what we might imagine.

THE SIDE EFFECTS OF PROBLEM DRINKING: RESILIENCE THEORY

Resiliency theory provides a framework for understanding the instances when events, labeled as stressors, result in outcomes that are not negative. Resilience as a concept emerged from studies of children who functioned competently after being exposed to adversity when psychopathology was expected (Garmezy, 1991; Hollister-Wagner et al., 2006; Masten, 1994; Werner & Smith, 1989). Simultaneously, researchers from many other disciplines were noting similar concepts. Antonovsky (1987), a medical sociologist, introduced a concept called *salutogenesis* to describe the high functioning of Holocaust survivors. Cassel (1976), an epidemiologist, introduced the term *host resistance* to describe factors that protect hosts from becoming ill even after being infected. This focus on positive adjustment to negative events also expanded to family studies, where McCubbin and Patterson (1982) observed that military families successfully adapted to the crises of war. Additionally, developmental psychologists, such as Rutter (1987) and Garmezy (1991), have recognized that among a plethora of groups known to be at high risk for developing difficulties, many individuals emerge unscathed by adversity. It is clear that various disciplines have made efforts to answer the question posed earlier: Are there instances where events that we have assumed are stressors result in effects in the opposite direction from what we might imagine? The phenomenon that is most often used to explain such instances is now called resilience.

Many studies on resiliency have naturally been focused on at-risk youth and their various responses to adversity. More specifically, scholars have begun to study resiliency in hopes of being better able to foster resiliency in children who are disproportionately placed at risk of academic failure. Children from poverty-stricken backgrounds (Natriello, McDill, & Pallas, 1990) and racial or cultural minority children (Gordon & Yowell, 1994; Natriello et al., 1990) have all been associated with academic risk. But, what causes an individual to be resilient?

The capacity for resilience varies and it may grow or decline over time depending on a number of factors, including the type and magnitude of the stressor, how it is perceived, and the skills and resources families or individuals have to cope with difficult experiences. All of these factors have the potential to mitigate otherwise negative effects of normatively stressful situations (Henderson & Milstein, 1996; Patterson, 2002). For example, just like family stress scholars, resilience scholars have noted that African Americans tend to have resources such as extended networks and social support that enable them to respond positively to adversity (Hall, 2008; Nicolas et al., 2008). Taken together, interest in at-risk youth and interest in uncovering factors that lead to their resiliency has prompted scholars to examine those children who face predisposition to failure, by way of risks and/or stressors, yet succeed. Borman and Overman (2004) found that for low-income students, greater engagement in academic activities, an internal locus of control, efficaciousness in math, a more positive outlook toward school, and a more positive self-esteem were all characteristics of students who achieved resilient mathematics outcomes.

Children of alcoholics have been used as one of the most prominent examples of resiliency amid a high-risk environment. Several researchers have identified the ability to separate oneself from a stressful family environment, to detach enough from parental distress to maintain outside pursuits and satisfactions, as the major characteristic of resilient children growing up in families with alcoholism (Benard, 1991; Berlin & Davis, 1989). In a sense, this literature on alcoholism stands opposed to literature on alcoholism that utilizes a family stress framework. As noted in the previous section, family stress theory suggests that stressors in the family lead to negative outcomes for children. However, this apparent point of diversion between the two theories may arguably represent a place where these two theories can come together to explain stressful experiences and a variety of outcomes, both positive and negative. Moreover, where family stress theory postulates that all families are prone to stressors, and that resources and perception dictate the adaptation the family makes to the stressor and how much of a negative effect this adaptation has on the children, resilience theory makes room for positive side effects. Taken together, these two theories allow us to view having a family history of problem drinking as a stressor that may result in decreased, stagnant, or increased educational attainment of children later in life.

METHODS

Hypotheses

The research presented in this chapter explores the effects of having a family history of problem drinking on children's education. The following models assess children's educational attainment as the outcome of interest. The results assess whether the presence of problem drinkers in the family acts as a stressor, exhibiting main effects on children's educational attainment and if this relationship is moderated by race. This research is guided by two hypotheses. In line with family stress theory, it was expected that having a family history of problem drinking would be associated with a decrease in educational attainment in aggregate analyses (Hypothesis 1). In line with resilience theory, wherein African Americans have greater resources and characteristics enabling resiliency, it is anticipated that race would moderate the relationship between having a family history of problem drinking and the educational attainment of children (Hypothesis 2) such that having a family history of problem drinking will have a stronger effect on White Americans compared to African Americans.

Data and measures

Data were extracted from the National Longitudinal Survey of Youth (NLSY) Mother and Young Adult (NLSY-YA) samples. The NLSY is a nationally representative sample of Americans and is part of a larger project sponsored by the U.S. Departments of Labor and Defense under a grant to the Center for Human Resource Research at the Ohio State University (Center for Human Resource Research, 2004). Respondents were interviewed annually from 1979 to 1994 and biennially after 1994. Initial ages ranged from 14 to 22 years old. In 1986, children born to the women of the NLSY sample were surveyed. These children have been interviewed biennially since 1986, collecting measures of cognitive ability, motor and social development, behavior problems, and quality of the home environment. In 1994 and every 2 years after, youth who were at least 15 years of age were surveyed separately (NLSY-YA) than those younger than 15. These data provided the ability to merge the data from the NLSY and NLSY-YA using the identification codes that link information about mother and child. From the NLSY-YA, information from the 2006 and 2010 waves of data were utilized. In the baseline year of this study (2006), the young adults were 21 to 34 years old and their mothers were 41 to 49 years old. With regard to this study, only complete case analyses ($N = 1,512$) are presented. There are 943 White Americans and 569 African Americans in the sample.

Dependent variable

There is one dependent variable for this study: educational attainment. The survey item on educational attainment queried the highest grade completed at the time of the survey. This measure is coded as 1 through 20 with each number corresponding to the number of years of education fully completed at the time the question was asked.

Independent and control variables

Independent variables: Family history of problem drinking and race. There are two independent variables in this study: (1) family history of problem drinking, the primary independent variable; and (2) race, the moderator. Utilizing the mother–child component of the NLSY and NLSY-YA, those having a relative with a drinking problem were coded as 1 if it was reported that their mother, father, or biological grandparents had a problem with alcohol use. This information came from the 1988 wave of the NLSY when respondents of this study were 3 to 16 years old and living in their mother's home. To the extent that race might affect or moderate one's response to a stressor, a separate dummy variable was created that distinguishes African Americans and compared them to Whites (reference group). All other races and ethnicities have been removed from this sample.

Control variables: Family characteristics, drug use, and demographic characteristics. In order to test whether family characteristics accounted for discrepancies in educational attainment, a number of control variables were used including mother's reliance on an extended kin network, mother's years of education, residence with biological parents at age 18, mother's experience with poverty, mother's marijuana use, and mother's crack use. The mother's use of an extended kin network was coded as 1 if the mother received free child care, if over half her income came from some person other than her spouse, or if she lived in a household with people over the age of 18 (adopted from Hogan, Hao, & Parish, 1990). To the extent that discrepancies in educational attainment might be affected by racial differences in the respondents own alcohol consumption and drug use (Barnes, Weite, & Hoffman, 2002), information on respondent drug use was collected. The measures included are the number of drinks a respondent has per occasion and whether the respondent indicated that they were a heavy drinker or marijuana smoker. Last, models presented in this chapter controlled for a number of demographic variables that are intuitively linked to educational attainment. The variables included were the respondents' age, sex, employment status, level of income, and marital status.

Analytic strategy

In order to determine the relationship between having a family history of problem drinking and educational attainment, and whether that relationship is moderated by race, a series of regression models were estimated using educational attainment (years of schooling completed) as the outcome variable of interest. The first model was a regression analysis that tested whether having a family history of problem drinking exhibited any main effects on educational attainment, only controlling for demographics where those variables are commonly associated with educational attainment. To be sure that this relationship was not impacted by external relationships, controls for family characteristics were then added into the model. Together, these two models test Hypothesis 1 that having a family history of problem drinking would be associated with a decrease in educational attainment. Next, a variable representing the status of being African American and an interaction variable for the status of being African American and having a family history of problem drinking were added to the model to test Hypothesis 2, that race would moderate the impact of having a family history of problem drinking on educational attainment. To be sure that this relationship was not impacted by the racial differences in alcohol and drug use (Barnes et al., 2002), controls for the respondents' current drinking and marijuana use were added to the model. Last, an indicator of whether the respondents' mothers relied on external social support was added to the model to test for within-group differences and to determine if this reliance explains away any of the potential differential affects of familial problem drinking on educational attainment.

Table 3.1 presents descriptive statistics for all study variables. In order to provide comparison to other educational inequality scholarship and highlight differences in the sample by race, the descriptive table splits the sample by race to compare characteristics. Over half the sample (62.37%) is White. The mean educational attainment is 12.86 years and there is no significant difference between Whites and African Americans. It is important to note that there are no significant differences between White Americans and African Americans

Table 3.1 Means, percentages, and standard deviations (SD) for all study variables

Variables	Total sample (n = 1,512)		White (n = 943)		African American (n = 569)	
	Mean or percent	SD	Mean or percent	SD	Mean or percent	SD
Dependent variables						
Education (years)	12.86	1.93	12.92	2.01	12.78	1.79
% Less than a high school[a]	17.46	–	18.66	–	15.47	–
% Completed high school	36.11		33.83		39.89*	
% More than a high school	46.43		47.51		44.64	
Independent and control variables						
Age (years)	22.88	3.71	22.30	3.52	23.84***	3.83
% Male	49.60	–	51.75	–	46.05*	–
% Employed	78.77		79.32		71.35***	
% Married	16.47		20.47		9.84***	
Income (logged thousands of dollars per year)	2.40	1.13	2.42	2.35	2.36	2.27
Respondent drug use						
% Heavy drinker or marijuana user	41.20	–	44.33	–	36.03**	–
# of drinks per day	2.79	2.69	3.21	3.02	2.08***	1.92
Family drug use						
% Parent/grandparent problem drinkers	26.39	–	27.47		24.60	

(Continued)

Table 3.1 (Continued) Means, percentages, and standard deviations (SD) for all study variables

Variables	Total sample (n = 1,512)		White (n = 943)		African American (n = 569)	
	Mean or percent	SD	Mean or percent	SD	Mean or percent	SD
Family characteristics						
Highest year of school completed by mother (years)	12.89	2.31	13.03	2.38	12.64**	2.16
% Raised with both biological parents	28.04	—	37.75	—	11.95***	—
% Parents experienced poverty	19.38		9.86		35.15***	
% Mother used marijuana	56.08		60.13		49.38***	
% Mother used crack	4.23		3.08		6.15**	
Extended kin network						
% Mother relied on kin network	35.54	—	29.72	—	43.80***	—

Notes: Asterisks denote significant differences between Whites and African Americans, where *p < .05, **p < .01, and ***p < .001.

a To gauge the representativeness of the sample, dummy variables were created, each corresponding to traditional education markers: less than a high school diploma (coded 1 if years of education <12), high school diploma (coded 1 if years of education =12), and more than a high school diploma (coded 1 if years of education >12). However, due to the fact that years of education completed do not directly correspond to these traditional education markers, analyses were not conducted utilizing these markers as dependent variables.

regarding the presence of familial problem drinking. Additional, it is note-worthy that African Americans report less drug use than Whites.

RESULTS

Correlations were conducted among all study variables separately for African Americans and Whites (not presented in this chapter). Of critical importance is the bivariate relationship between having a family history of problem drinking and educational attainment for both Whites and African Americans. For African Americans, there is a small, positive relationship, meaning the status of having a family history of problem drinking is associated with an increase in educational attainment ($r = .13, p < .01$). For Whites, there is no significant relationship between family history of problem drinking and educational attainment ($r = -.05, p =$ n.s.). These bivariate relationships suggest that there may be differential effects of familial problem drinking on educational attainment between the two groups of respondents.

Table 3.2 presents the ordinary least squares regression results for educational attainment, which explores the differential effects in more depth. Model 1 confirms that, in the aggregate, there is no significant relationship between educational attainment and having a family history of problem drinking. Model 2 includes controls for certain family characteristics to determine whether there are any variables that could be related to familial problem drinking and educational attainment, and, thus, explain the relationship between the two. Mother's education and living with both biological parents are both associated with an increase in educational attainment. The status of having a mother who experienced poverty and used marijuana are both associated with decreases in educational attainment. There is still no significant relationship between having a family history of problem drinking and educational attainment. Model 3 includes the status of being African American and an interaction term representing those individuals who are African American and have a family history of problem drinking. After controlling for differences in respondents drug use, Model 3 demonstrates that race moderates the relationship between having a family history of problem drinking and educational attainment. Though the status of being African American is associated with a decrease in educational attainment, compared to Whites, and having a family history of problem drinking weakens this negative association. In Model 4, controls are added for mother's reliance on an extended kin network. In this model, the mother's reliance on an extended kin network is positively associated with respondents' later educational attainment. Additionally, after including this variable as a control, the strength of the association between educational attainment and the status of being African American with a family history of problem drinking is reduced.

In terms of the hypotheses, Model 1 and Model 2 demonstrate that there is no support for Hypothesis 1 that having a family history of problem drinking

Table 3.2 Educational attainment regressed on selected independent variables and interactions; National Longitudinal Survey of Youth–Young Adult Sample (N = 1,512)

Independent variables	Model 1		Model 2		Model 3		Model 4	
	b	se	b	se	b	se	b	se
Family history of problem drinking (1 = yes)	.00	.10	.10	.10	−.15	.13	−.13	.12
Control								
Age (years)	.12***	.01	.16***	.01	.17***	.02	.16***	.01
Male (1 = yes)	−.52***	.09	−.57***	.09	−.51***	.09	−.53***	.09
Employed (1 = yes)	.60***	.11	.43***	.11	.41***	.10	.41***	.10
Married (1 = yes)	−.02	.13	−.03	.13	−.11	.13	−.13	.13
Income (logged)	.35***	.05	.35***	.05	.34***	.05	.30***	.05
Family characteristics								
Highest grade completed by mother (years)			.15***	.02	.15***	.02	.16***	.02
Living with biological parents at 18 (1 = yes)			.41***	.11	.37***	.11	.33**	.11
Mother experienced poverty (1 = yes)			−.41***	.12	−.36***	.12	−.30**	.12
Mother used marijuana (1 = yes)			−.30**	.09	−.30**	.09	−.31***	.09
Mother used crack (1 = yes)			.21	.22	.22	.22	.25	.22
African American (1 = yes)					−.40***	.12	−.40***	.12
African American × Family history of problem drinking					.66**	.21	.49*	.20

(Continued)

Table 3.2 (Continued) Educational attainment regressed on selected independent variables and interactions: National Longitudinal Survey of Youth–Young Adult Sample (N = 1,512)

Independent variables	Model 1		Model 2		Model 3		Model 4	
	b	se	b	se	b	se	b	se
Respondent drug use								
# of drinks per occasion					−.05**	.02	−.04*	.02
Heavy drinker or marijuana smoker (1 = yes)					.04	.10	.06	.10
Extended kin network								
Mother relied on extended kin network (1 = yes)							.07**	.02
Constant	9.11		6.42		6.55		4.09	
Adj R squared	.16		.23		.23		.25	

Note: *p < .05, **p < .01, and ***p < .001.

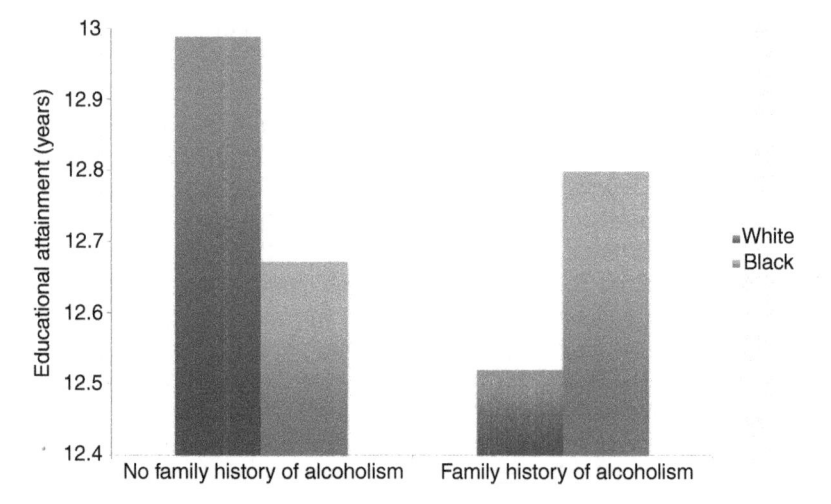

Figure 3.1 Interaction graph for having a family history of problem drinking and race on educational attainment.

would be associated with a decrease in educational attainment. However, Model 3 and Model 4 support Hypothesis 2 that race would moderate the relationship between having a family history of problem drinking and the educational attainment of children. Further, Model 3 and Model 4 provide insight into the lack of support for Hypothesis 1. Since Model 1 and Model 2 include both African Americans and Whites in comparing the educational attainment of those with a family history of problem drinking to those without, the lack of relationship for Whites hides the positive relationship for African Americans. Figure 3.1 is a graphic representation of the interaction depicted in Model 4.

DISCUSSION AND CONCLUSION

This chapter extends existing understandings of potential threats to educational attainment by exploring the effects of having a family history of alcohol overconsumption as a stressor on the longitudinal adjustment of youth. Specifically, this chapter provides insight into whether and how race explains the relationship between having a family history of problem drinking and the educational attainment of children. The results presented in this chapter are fruitful in three ways.

First, it appears that having a family history of problem drinking is not linked to educational attainment for Whites after controlling for a host of other characteristics, but having a family history of problem drinking is positively associated with educational attainment for African Americans. If this study solely utilized family stress theory, treating the presence of family problem drinking as a universal stressor, and, thus not disaggregating by race, one might have erroneously assumed that the lack of a main effect was reason to dismiss familial problem drinking as a stressor. However, the findings of these studies suggest that experiencing problem drinking in the family is not universal and does not have universal effects. Further, the findings presented here corroborate research that demonstrates that some individuals are either unscathed by or resilient to the stresses created by having a family history of problem drinking (Benard, 1991; Berlin & Davis, 1989). These findings also corroborate research that posits that African American children are more resilient in the face of adversity (Borman & Overman, 2004; Nicolas, 2008).

In a family stress framework, one might assume that the presence of problem drinking in the family causes psychological distress to family members, including children, and this distress would result in decreased ability to function adequately in school. This assumption guided the hypothesis that having a family history of family drinking would be associated with a decrease in educational attainment. However, this hypothesis was not supported. Family stress theory remained a possible explanation as some researchers have observed that social support and other resources serve as a buffer to stressors, allowing families to be unaffected by stressors (Belsky, 1984; Murry et al., 2001). However, results demonstrate that family stress theory might not provide the best explanation for problem drinking in the family.

Resilience theory provides a framework for understanding the instances when events, labeled as stressors, result in outcomes that are not negative. Utilizing resilience theory, researchers have found that many people respond positively to growing up with alcoholic parents (Benard, 1991; Berlin & Davis, 1989). Researchers have also found that African American children are resilient in many normatively stressful situations (Borman & Overman, 2004; Nicolas, 2008). Within the framework of resilience theory, one might assume that the presence of alcoholism in the families of African American children may result in an increase in educational attainment due to their abundance of social support and resources outside of their immediate family. This assumption guided the hypothesis that race would moderate the relationship between having a family history of problem drinking and the educational attainment of children. The results indicate that African Americans are resilient to having a family history of problem drinking such that the negative effect of being African American on educational attainment is overcompensated for by the presence of this stressor.

Notwithstanding the strengths of this study, the results are limited in a few respects. First, a measure of alcohol consumption that is linked to but not a direct measure of clinically diagnosed alcoholism was used. This self-report of alcohol consumption may account for discrepancies with results from previous studies. Next, social support and social resources, which are critical components of both theories, may not adequately be controlled for in this model. Though it is plausible that the variables used here serve as legitimate proxies for social support and resources, other data sets may provide direct measures of these aspects of individuals' lives. The age range of this sample is 21 to 34 years old at baseline; though the intergenerational linkage of the two data sets used in this sample is key, the time between measurements of mother's indication of problem drinking in the family and children's educational attainment may be a source of some discrepancy. Next, a complete mechanism by which these African American children positively respond to the presence of alcohol overconsumption in the family was not found. Including the extent to which mothers relied on external support in the models did reduce the strength of the relationship between the key interaction and the dependent variable. However, it did not completely explain away the differential impact of familial problem drinking between Whites and African Americans. It is quite plausible that the person upon whom the mother relies for social support is a grandparent, who, in this study, may be a problem drinker himself or herself. Last, this study examines educational attainment as the outcome of interest. While contributions to the understanding of how far students progress in the educational system are important, educational attainment is not directly correlated with academic achievement (i.e., GPA [grade point average], test scores, and concomitant differential college acceptance). Furthermore, though the findings presented in this chapter demonstrate that African Americans with problem drinking family members go further in school than Whites who also have problem drinking family members and African Americans who are not in problem drinking families, questions remain regarding whether this same pattern holds true for their academic achievement. These limitations hamper the generalizability of the findings presented here but provide avenues for future researchers to more fully develop the mechanisms by which individuals or groups of individuals bounce back from adversity.

In conclusion, previous research on alcoholism in the family has fallen on two drastically different sides. One side understands alcoholism as an impairment to psychological functioning and resulting in negative child outcomes (Reich et al., 2006). Other research suggests that individuals are resilient to the stressor of having a family history of alcoholism (Benard, 1991; Berlin & Davis, 1989). Family stress theory and resilience theory, respectively, support each of these claims. Although few studies have examined how having a family history of alcoholism is different for African American children and White children, the results of this chapter suggest that African American children are resilient in the face of this stressor. Moreover, this study aligns with resilience theory with respect to problem drinking in the family but only for African American children. Despite the fact that children of alcoholics are only 25% likely to become alcoholics themselves, some may believe that the presence of alcoholism interferes with child development. This belief may cause people to assume that children raised in alcoholic families are at risk of underperformance and underachievement in schools. However, as demonstrated here, the adversity posed by the overconsumption of alcohol in the family is associated with higher educational attainment for one group of children. Thus, the label "at risk" does not fit. There are likely other situations in which scholars, clinicians, teachers, parents, and others have labeled people in "stressful" situations as "at risk," not recognizing that the presence of a stressor may not impact some groups and cause others to utilize resources that allow them to thrive.

This research is in line with the push for schools and clinicians to tap into the characteristics that make children resilient in the face of adversity and begin to foster resiliency (Benard, 1991; Williams, Mohammed, Leavell, & Collins, 2010). Further, after uncovering specific mechanisms for children's resiliency, if we imagine that resiliency is a gene that all children have, schools, parents, community organizations, and so forth may need to learn how to turn that gene on. One such mechanism is the family. However, the family is not the only answer. Though the mechanism may vary for different groups of children, learning to effectively turn on the resiliency gene may result in a collapsing of the achievement gap that has longed plagued our society.

REFERENCES

Anderson, K. (2002). Perpetrator or victim? Relationships between intimate partner violence and well-being. *Journal of Marriage and Family, 64*, 851–863.

Antonovsky, A. (1987). *Unraveling the mystery of health.* San Francisco: Jossey-Bass.

Barnes, G., Weite, J., & Hoffman, J. (2002). Relationship of alcohol use to delinquency and illicit drug use in adolescents: Gender, age, and racial/ethnic differences. *Journal of Drug Issues, 32*(2), 153–178.

Belsky, J. (1984). The determinants of parenting: A process model. *Child Development, 55*, 83–96.

Benard, B. (1991). *Fostering resiliency in kids: Protective factors in the family, school, and community.* Portland, OR: Western Center for Drug-Free Schools and Communities.

Berlin, R., & Davis, R. (1989). Children from alcoholic families: Vulnerability and resilience. In T. Dugan & R. Coles (Eds.), *The child in our times: Studies in the development of resiliency.* New York: Brunner-Mazel.

Borman, G., & Overman, T. (2004). Academic resilience in mathematics among poor and minority students. *The Elementary School Journal, 104*(3), 177–195.

Cassel, J. (1976). The contribution of the social environment to host resistance. *American Journal of Epidemiology, 104*(2), 107–123.

Center for Human Resource Research. (2004). NLSY79 *child and young adult: Data user's guide: A guide to the 1979 National Longitudinal Survey of Youth 1979; 1986–2002 child data; 1994–2002 young adult data.* Columbus, OH: Ohio State University.

Conger, R., Conger, K., Elder, G., Lorenz, F., Simons, R., & Whitbeck, L. (1992). A family process model of economic hardship and adjustment of early adolescent boys. *Child Development, 63*(3), 526–541.

Conger, R., Ge, X., Elder, G., Lorenz, F., & Simon, R. (1994). Economic stress, coercive process, and developmental problems of adolescents. *Child Development, 65*, 541–561.

Elder, G., Liker, J., & Cross, C. (1984). Parent-child behavior in the Great Depression: Life course and intergenerational influences. In P. Bates & O. Brim (Eds.), *Lifespan development and behavior* (Vol. 6, pp. 109–158). New York: Academic Press.

Elder, G., Nguyen, T., & Capsi, A. (1985). Linking family hardship to children's lives. *Child Development, 56*(2), 361–375.

Garmezy, N. (1991). Resiliency and vulnerability to adverse developmental outcomes associated with poverty. *American Behavioral Scientist, 34*(2), 416–430.

Gordon, E. W., & Yowell, C. (1994). Educational reforms for students at risk: Cultural dissonance as a risk factor in the development of students. In R. Rossi (Ed.), *Educational reforms and students at risk* (pp. 51–69). New York: Teachers College Press.

Hall, J. (2008). The impact of kin and fictive relationships on the mental health of Black adult children of alcoholics. *Health and Social Work, 33*(4), 259–266.

Henderson, N., & Milstein, M. M. (1996). *Resiliency in schools: Making it happen for students and educators*. Thousand Oaks, CA: Corwin.

Hogan, D., Hao, L., & Parish, W. (1990). Race, kin networks, and assistance to mother-headed families. *Social Forces, 68*(3), 797–812.

Hollister-Wagner, G., Foshee, V., & Jackson, C. (2006). Adolescent aggression: Models of resiliency. *Journal of Applied Psychology, 31*(3), 445–466.

Kotchick, B., Dorsey, S., & Heller, L. (2005). Predictors of parenting among African American single mothers: Personal and contextual factors. *Journal of Marriage & Family, 67*(2), 448–460.

Masten, A. (1994). Resilience in individual development: Successful adaptation despite risk and adversity. In M. Wang & E. Gordon (Eds.), *Educational resilience in inner-city America: Challenges and prospects* (pp. 3–25). Hillsdale, NJ: Erlbaum.

Mannino, C., & Deutsch, F. (2007). Changing the division of household labor: A negotiated process between partners. *Sex Roles, 56*, 309–324.

McCord, J. (1972). Etiological factors in alcoholism: Family and personal characteristics. *Quarterly Journal of Studies on Alcohol, 33*(4), 1020–1027.

McCubbin, H., & Patterson, J. (1982). Family adaptation to crises. In H. McCubbin, A. Cauble, & J. Patterson (Eds.), *Family stress, coping and social support*. Springfield, IL: C.C. Thomas.

McLoyd, C., Jayaratne, T., Ceballo, R., & Borquez, J. (1994). Unemployment and work interruptions among African American single mothers: Effects on parenting and adolescent socioemotional functioning. *Child Development, 65*, 562–589.

Murry, V., Bynum, M., Brody, G., Willert, A., & Stephens, D. (2001). African American single mothers and children in context: A review of studies on risk and resilience. *Clinical Child and Family Psychology Review, 4*(1), 133–155.

Nardi, P. (1981). Children of alcoholics: A role-theoretical perspective. *The Journal of Social Psychology, 115*(2), 237–245.

Natriello, G., McDill, E., & Pallas, A. (1990). *Schooling disadvantaged children: Racing against catastrophe*. New York: Teachers College Press.

Nicolas, G., Helms, J., Jernigan, M., Sass, T., Skrzypek, A., & DeSilva, A. (2008). A conceptual framework for understanding the strengths of African American Youths. *The Journal of African American Psychology, 34*(2), 261–280.

Patterson, J. (2002). Integrating family resilience and family stress theory. *Journal of Marriage and Family, 64*(2), 349–360.

Reich, W., Earls, F., & Powell, J. (2006). A comparison of the home and social environments of children of alcoholic and non-alcoholic parents. *British Journal of Addiction, 83*(7), 831–839.

Rutter, M. (1987). Parental mental disorder as a psychiatric risk factor. In R. Hales & A. Frances (Eds.), *American Psychiatric Association Annual Review* (Vol. 6, pp. 647–663). Washington, DC: American Psychological Association.

Wang, H., & Amato, P. (2000). Predictors of divorce adjustment: Stressors, resources, and definitions. *Journal of Marriage and Family, 62*(2), 655–668.

Werner, E., & Smith, R. (1989). *Vulnerable but invincible: A longitudinal study of resilient children and youth.* New York: Adams, Bannister, & Cox.

Williams, D. R., Mohammed, S. A., Leavell, J., & Collins, C. (2010). Race, socioeconomic status, and health: Complexities, ongoing challenges, and research opportunities. *Annals of the New York Academy of Sciences, 1186*(1), 69–101.

4 Lifetime mental disorders and education experiences among Black adolescents

Theda Rose, Nadine M. Finigan-Carr, and Sean Joe

Within the literature on mental health and educational experiences among youth, little attention has been paid to the factors that influence Black students' success or failure outside of cultural stereotypes as the inferior minority (Whaley & Noel, 2013). African American adolescents' successful transition to adulthood is contingent on their academic achievement, employable skill and abilities, and their physical and mental health. This chapter reviews the literature on Black adolescents' mental health problems, their educational experiences, and information about the relationship between mental health and educational experiences among adolescents. The chapter then provides data on the relationship between mental disorders and educational experiences among Black adolescents, specifically.

MENTAL HEALTH PROBLEMS AMONG BLACK ADOLESCENTS

Adolescence is marked by many social, cognitive, and physical changes (Peterson & Hamburg, 1986). Development among children and adolescents are shaped by continuous exchanges with others in family, peer, and other cultural environments. These environments in addition to personal factors have the potential to influence adolescent mental health (e.g., Rose, Joe, Shields, & Caldwell, 2014; Rowling, 2006). Consistent with the general population of adolescents, Black adolescents are overall resilient; they are, however, at greater risk for adverse psychosocial outcomes due to their overrepresentation in resource-poor environments (e.g., poor living conditions, inferior schools) (Gibbs, 1990; Myers, 1989; Rosella & Albrecht, 1993). Prior research shows that Black adolescents experience significant mental health problems (e.g., lifetime rates of 55% for any disorder including mood, anxiety, substance, and impulse disorders) (Kessler et al., 2012) and are less represented in mental health research (U.S. Department of Health & Human Services, 2001), which limits our understanding about mental health problems among this subset of adolescents.

Negative characteristics of low socioeconomic environments, such as community violence, poverty, and deviant peer groups, may further contribute to adverse mental health outcomes for African American adolescents. For example, studies focused on poverty as a context for mental health status showed that poverty was significantly related to mental disorders (e.g., McLaughlin et al., 2011). Concomitantly, studies show that African American adolescents may be at higher risk for adverse mental health outcomes, such as depression (Lambert, Herman, Bynum, & Ialongo, 2009), and may report greater psychiatric problems and greater risk of comorbid mental health problems (Chen, Killeya-Jones, & Vega, 2005) as compared to other racial/ethnic groups. A significant body of work has outlined the harmful effects of racism on both the physical and mental health of adult African Americans. Specifically, racism has been linked to adverse birth outcomes, substance use and abuse, hypertension, cancer, and psychological functioning. Chapter 3 has contributed to this discussion specifically for African American children from birth throughout development, especially with regard to the classroom. However, comparatively few studies have examined the impact of racism on African American adolescents' mental health outcomes. Though limited, these studies have documented associations between experiences with racism and discrimination with adolescents' poorer mental health outcomes, including general psychological distress, externalizing and internalizing behaviors, and substance use (Lambert et al., 2009).

EDUCATIONAL EXPERIENCES AMONG BLACK ADOLESCENTS AND THE INFLUENCE OF MENTAL HEALTH PROBLEMS

Schools in inner-city neighborhoods are typically characterized by economic disadvantage, less social cohesion, and fewer resources for educating children when compared to suburban schools, all of which potentially contribute to more negative educational trajectories (e.g., Basch, 2011; Ceballo, McLoyd, & Toyokawa, 2004; Clayton, 2011). These schools also tend to have a disproportionately less diverse student body, suffer from a lack of qualified and effective teachers, and provide less access to higher-level learning opportunities (Clayton, 2011; Jacob, 2007; Levin, 2009), which can consequentially impact better educational outcomes. This may be particularly significant for Black adolescents, who are disproportionately represented in schools where more than half the students live in poverty (Orfield & Lee, 2005).

In all, nearly 1 million students, or 2.3% of those enrolled, were retained across K–12 in the United States. Nationwide data collected by the U.S. Department of Education's Office for Civil Rights reveal stark racial and ethnic disparities in student retentions, with African American students far more likely than White students to repeat a grade, especially in elementary and middle school (Adams, Robelen, & Shah, 2012). Although African American students represented less than one-fifth of the United States K–12 students, they were nearly 3 times as likely as White students to be retained, when combining all grade levels (Adams et al., 2012). Retention is likely related to graduation rate and other education achievement outcomes. Additionally, Aud, Fox, and Kewal Ramani (2010) reported that during 2007, a higher percentage (43%) of Black students in grades 6–12 had been suspended from school at some point compared to any other racial/ethnic group.

African American youth have a qualitatively different experience in public schools compared to White youth, particularly in underresourced communities. When Black students are in classrooms with fewer resources and an increased focus of the teachers on discipline rather than instruction, their academic achievement suffers (Davis & Jordan, 1994). Inadequate resources may lead school professionals to focus solely on children's behavior, without also addressing underlying affective symptoms, such as depression, and related attitudes, such as low academic engagement. These school level factors can also place youth within these communities at an increased risk for aggressive and other externalizing behavior (Bradshaw, Sawyer, & O'Brennan, 2009; Greene, 2005). Bullying tends to be more of a problem as well. Several school-related problems have been associated with bullying, including low academic readiness, school failure, decreased school engagement, school dropout, suspension, and mobility (Bradshaw, Waasdorp, Goldweber, & Johnson, 2013). Many of these behavioral problems lead to disciplinary action. This may reflect unmet mental health needs, especially for African American youth (Brady, Winston, & Gockley, 2014). However, there is also the potential for mental health problems for African American students who excel academically because due to racism and discrimination there is the perception that they are not the norm (Whaley & Noel, 2013). Black youth may also experience emotional distress in association with social problems, such as school withdrawal and low academic tracking (Gibbs, 1990; Rosella & Albrecht, 1993; Thompson & Massat, 2005).

Studies that examined the relationship between mental health problems and educational outcomes generally showed a negative educational trajectory for those reporting mental health problems (e.g., Ansary & Luthar, 2009; Dubow, Huesmann, Boxer, Pulkkinen, & Kokko, 2006; Serbin et al., 2011). For example, McLeod and Fettes (2007) report that high levels of internalizing and externalizing problems in childhood or adolescence are related to poorer educational attainment in young adulthood. Similarly, depression was related to lower academic achievement among junior and high school students (Rothon, Head, Klineberg, & Stansfeld, 2011; Weist, Wong, & Kreil, 1998) and children displaying externalizing problems such as aggression and antisocial behaviors show grade retention difficulties in school (Nagin, Pagani, Tremblay, & Vitaro, 2003).

Educational attainment is the aspect of development with the most significance for adolescents' future lives. The more years of education one receives the better one's chances of success in multiple domains, such as employment, occupational status, income, housing, and marriage. However, African American students appear to be less prepared to become healthy, productive, and successful adults than their peers in this regard. They tend to have difficulty completing school at each stage of the pipeline from early childhood through high school. This results in reduced attempts at college and difficulty in finding employment. In addition, African American adolescents may manifest poor mental health, which makes successful transition to adulthood difficult. Though studies exist on the relationship between mental health problems and educational outcomes among youth in general, we know less about this relationship among Black adolescents. Thus, we examine that next. Specifically, we explore (a) the prevalence of mental disorders and educational experiences among Black youth, overall and by gender, and (b) the association between mental health and education experiences.

CURRENT STUDY

Study design, sampling, and data collection

Data from the adolescent sample of the 2001–2003 National Survey of American Life (NSAL) (Jackson et al., 2004) were used to examine our study questions. Researchers at the Program for Research on Black Americans through the University of Michigan's Institute for Social Research conducted the study over the course of two years (February 2001–June 2003). The NSAL is an institutional review board (IRB)–approved nationally representative household survey that utilized a stratified and clustered sample design to obtain a nationally representative sample of 3,570 African Americans (AAs), 1,006 non-Hispanic Whites, and 1,621 Blacks of Caribbean descent (CBs) aged 18 years and older (see Jackson et al., 2004, for more information on the NSAL). Every AA and CB household that included an adult participant in the NSAL was assessed for an eligible adolescent living in the household to produce the NSAL-Adolescent sample (NSAL-A). Adolescents were then selected using a randomized procedure. If more than one adolescent in the household was suitable, up to two adolescents were selected to participate, and, where possible, the second adolescent was of a different gender (Sweetman et al., 2009). Before the interview, informed consent was obtained from the adolescent's legal guardian and assent from the adolescent. Only AA and CB adolescents were interviewed (see Joe, Baser, Neighbors, Caldwell, & Jackson, 2009, for more detailed information about the NSAL-A).

Measures

Mental disorders

Adolescent study participants completed a diagnostic interview using a modified version of the World Mental Health Composite International Diagnostic Interview (WMH-CIDI), which was based on the World Health Organization Composite International Diagnostic Interview (WHO-CIDI) (Kessler & Ustun, 2004). For the NSAL-A study, the instrument administered to the adolescents was adapted from the original version of the WMH-CIDI to accommodate youth as young as 13 years old (Sweetman et al., 2009). The fully structured diagnostic interview is lay-administered and generates classifications of psychiatric disorders as defined by the *Diagnostic and Statistical Manual of Mental Disorders*, 4th edition (*DSM-IV*) and the International Statistical Classification of Diseases, 10th revision (Andrews & Peters, 1998). The NSAL-A sample assessed five main categories of disorders, which includes 19 core *DSM-IV* mental disorders. The study provided information on anxiety disorders (generalized anxiety disorder, panic disorder, social phobia, agoraphobia, and posttraumatic stress disorder), mood disorders (major depressive disorder, dysthymia, irritable major depression, and bipolar I & II), substance disorders (alcohol abuse, alcohol dependence, drug abuse, and drug dependence), impulse control disorders (oppositional-defiant disorder, conduct disorder, and intermittent explosive disorder), and eating disorders (anorexia, bulimia, and binge eating disorder) (Sweetman et al., 2009). Previous research has demonstrated the CIDI to have good psychometric properties with adolescents as young as 15 years old (Andrews & Peters, 1998). The NSAL-A sample generated lifetime, 12-month, and 3-day *DSM-IV* diagnoses for each of the disorders. For the purpose of the present study, the lifetime diagnosis summary variable (with binge) will be used to indicate whether a respondent met the criteria for any anxiety, mood, impulse, substance abuse, or eating disorder. The variable is coded 0 = no disorder and 1 = one or more disorders.

Education variables

Grades are measured by asking the adolescent about the kind of grades s/he usually receives: mostly A's, mostly B's, mostly C's, mostly D's, or mostly failing grades. Grade retention is measured by the question, "Did you ever stay back or repeat a grade in school?" with a response of yes or no. Suspension is measured by the question, "Were you ever suspended from school for a day or longer?" with a response of yes or no. Expulsion is measured by the question, "Were you ever expelled from school?" with a response of yes or no.

Demographics

Demographics examined included gender, ethnicity (based on the race of the adult in the household; African American and Caribbean Black), and income. Income was coded in four ranges ($0–$17,999; $18,000–$31,999; $32,000–$54,999; and $55,000 and above).

Analysis

All analyses were conducted using IBM SPSS 22, accounting for the complex survey design. Frequencies and chi-square tests of association are used to describe the sample and examine relationships between mental health and educational outcomes, respectively. The design-corrected Rao-Scott adjusted chi-square statistic is reported, thus statistical significance for this analysis is based on the design-adjusted F and its degrees of freedom.

RESULTS

The sample consisted of 1170 AA and CB adolescents, ages 13 to 17. Descriptive information about the sample is provided in Table 4.1. There are a similar number of male and female adolescents, and the majority of youth fell into the $0–$31,999 income range.

Table 4.2 shows the prevalence of the mental health and education variables for the total sample and by gender. Approximately 37% of youth, overall, had experienced a mental disorder at some point during their lives. Over half the youth (59%) reported getting mostly A's and B's in school. Twenty-nine percent had repeated a grade and about 58% had ever been suspended for at least a day. The majority of youth overall (92.5%) had never been expelled. The chi-square analysis showed significant differences among all the study variables, except lifetime disorder, by gender. Girls had a higher percentage of A's and B's (71%) than boys (48%), $\chi^2 = 37.19$, $p = .000$. More boys repeated a grade (37%) than girls (21.6%), $\chi^2 = 33.93$, $p = .000$. Boys also had been

Table 4.1 Demographic characteristics of the National Survey of American Life Adolescent sample ($n = 1170$)

	n^a	$\%wt^b$	95% CI
Gender			
Male	563	50.0	46.5–63.5
Female	607	50.0	46.5–63.5
Ethnicity			
African American	810	93.4	91.9–94.6
Caribbean Black	360	6.6	5.4–8.1
Household income[c]			
$0–$17,999	244	30.2	27.7 (2.5)
$18,000–$31,999	223	27.6	27.4 (1.8)
$32,000–$54,999	187	23.2	24.6 (2.4)
≥$55,000	153	19.0	20.2 (2.2)

Notes: All weighted estimates are weighted to be nationally representative of the given population and subpopulations in the contiguous 48 states of the United States.
a Sample size (n) is unweighted.
b Unweighted.
c Reflects adult respondents' status.

Table 4.2 Prevalence of mental disorders and education outcomes among Black youth: Total sample and by gender

	Total sample		Male		Female		Characteristic × Gender χ^2
	n^a	$\%wt^b$	n^a	$\%wt^b$	n^a	$\%wt^b$	
Lifetime disorder							
Yes	431	36.6 (2.1)	214	39.0 (2.9)	217	34.3 (2.3)	$\chi^2 = 2.47,$
No	738	63.4 (2.1)	349	61.0 (2.9)	389	65.7 (2.3)	$p = .124$
Grades							
A's and B's	704	59.5 (2.2)	274	48.3 (3.5)	430	70.7 (1.9)	$\chi^2 = 37.19,$ $p = .000$
C's and below	458	40.5 (2.2)	282	51.7 (3.5)	176	29.3 (1.9)	
Ever repeated grade							
Yes	327	29.1 (2.6)	202	36.5 (3.5)	125	21.6 (2.2)	$\chi^2 = 33.93,$
No	843	70.9 (2.6)	361	63.5 (3.5)	482	78.4 (2.2)	$p = .000$
Ever suspended							
Yes	615	57.8 (1.7)	360	68.0 (2.5)	255	47.6 (2.7)	$\chi^2 = 24.09,$
No	555	42.2 (1.7)	203	32.0 (2.5)	352	52.4 (2.7)	$p = .000$
Ever expelled							
Yes	82	7.5 (0.8)	60	11.1 (1.4)	22	3.9 (1.0)	$\chi^2 = 12.99,$
No	1088	92.5 (0.8)	503	88.9 (1.4)	585	96.1 (1.0)	$p = .001$

Notes: All weighted estimates are weighted to be nationally representative of the given population and subpopulations in the contiguous 48 states of the United States. Standard errors and χ^2 statistics are adjusted for the sampling stratification, clustering and weighting of the data.
a   Sample size (n) is unweighted.
b   Weighted (standard error).

suspended more often (68% versus 48%), $\chi^2 = 24.09$, $p = .000$; and had higher expulsion rates (11%) than girls (3.9%), $\chi^2 = 12.99$, $p = .001$.

Table 4.3 presents the findings of chi-square analysis of lifetime mental disorder and education variables. Results show a statistically significant association between lifetime any disorder and all of the educational outcomes. Youth reporting a lifetime disorder had fewer A's and B's, $\chi^2 = 5.23$, $p = .028$; and greater incidences of repeating a grade, $\chi^2 = 7.03$, $p = .011$ than those without a disorder. Interestingly, those reporting a disorder had more A's and B's than C's and D's. Further, youth with greater incidence of disorder had more suspensions, $\chi^2 = 12.58$, $p = .001$ and expulsions, $\chi^2 = 18.22$, $p = .000$ from school compared to those reporting no disorder.

Table 4.3 Lifetime mental disorders and educational outcomes among Black youth

	Lifetime mental disorders				Lifetime mental disorders × Education outcomes
	Yes		No		
	n^a	$\%wt^b$	n^a	$\%wt^b$	χ^2
Grades					
A's and B's	230	53.1 (3.7)	473	63.2 (2.5)	$\chi^2 = 5.23, p = .028$
C's and below	199	46.9 (3.7)	259	36.8 (2.5)	
Ever repeated grade					
Yes	141	35.1 (3.5)	186	25.6 (2.9)	$\chi^2 = 7.03, p = .011$
No	290	64.9 (3.5)	552	74.4 (2.9)	
Ever suspended					
Yes	279	68.6 (2.9)	335	51.5 (2.7)	$\chi^2 = 12.58, p = .001$
No	152	31.4 (2.9)	403	48.5 (2.7)	
Ever expelled					
Yes	47	11.6 (1.5)	35	5.1 (0.8)	$\chi^2 = 18.22, p = .000$
No	384	88.4 (1.5)	703	94.9 (0.8)	

Notes: All weighted estimates are weighted to be nationally representative of the given population and subpopulations in the contiguous 48 states of the United States. Standard errors and χ^2 statistics are adjusted for the sampling stratification, clustering, and weighting of the data.
a   Sample size (n) is unweighted.
b   Weighted (standard error).

DISCUSSION AND CONCLUSION

This chapter examined the relationship between mental health problems and education experiences among Black youth. As discussed, though Black adolescents, like the general population of adolescents, are resilient, they are at higher risk for experiencing mental health problems and qualitatively poorer educational outcomes than other subgroups of adolescents, due, in part, to their overrepresentation in resource-poor environments. Though research does exist on the link between mental health and education experiences among youth in general, this chapter seeks to reduce this dearth of literature on these relationships among Black adolescents. Thus, the study was an important step in our understanding of these relationships among this understudied group.

The educational experiences of Black adolescents remain a public health issue. These adolescents tend to be disproportionately represented in schools that lack the financial and qualified personnel resources critical to a successful learning experience, placing them at risk for poorer educational trajectories (e.g., Basch, 2011). From our data we observe that around 40% of Black youth report grades of C or below and close to one-third are repeating a grade. Over half have been suspended, but the majority has not been expelled. The picture changes somewhat when looking at differences between boys and girls. Black boys are having a poorer school experience, getting lower grades, repeating grades more often, and reporting more suspensions and expulsions than girls. Though not explored here, negative peer influences may play a role. According to Noguera (2003), peers particularly influence male stance toward achievement and their concept of identity in the school setting. Thus, alignment with a chosen peer group may influence choices, positive or negative, around school engagement and achievement as part of identity development at school (e.g., Ryan, 2000).

Mental health among Black adolescents is influenced by a number of factors (e.g., family, peers, discrimination). Though not examined directly, we can surmise that the prevalence rates that we describe are influenced by a number of complex and likely interacting environmental factors, as there is a constant exchange between adolescents and their environments. Kessler et al. (2012) reported a 55% prevalence rate of any disorder among Black adolescents. Though not as high, the rate we report is still quite alarming. More than one-third of the adolescents in this sample (37%) have, over the course of their lifetime, experienced some form of disorder (e.g., depression, anxiety). At the same time as these young people are navigating the normal changes in adolescence, they are also struggling with a mental health problem, which has the potential to affect other areas of their development, like their education. Our research found that having a lifetime disorder was significantly associated with a poorer educational trajectory compared to not having a disorder evidenced by fewer A's and B's, and higher incidences of retention, suspensions, and expulsions. Consistent with the results for adolescents on a whole, based on other studies (e.g., Rothon et al., 2011), the same negative trend is observed.

Though there are potentially important results, there are some limitations to our interpretations. The data is primarily self-reported, and the data set is cross-sectional, so we cannot state causality or discuss direction of the relationships. More objective measures of education outcomes should be used in future studies to confirm the putative association of the current study. Future research should examine whether those with mental health problems are more likely to experience poor education outcomes or whether adolescents who struggle in school may be more susceptible to a mental health problem. Additionally, further examination of gender trends, as well as differences by ethnicity is warranted. Finally, other potential influences on the relationship between mental health problems and educational outcomes should be directly examined.

In summary, many factors have the potential to influence important adolescent development outcomes, like their education. Among Black youth, who may experience poorer educational trajectories, mental health problems emerge as an important factor. Our data suggests that youth with mental health problems may be more susceptible to poorer educational trajectories. Teachers and other school personnel must consider a student's mental illness, when developing individual education plans or addressing externalizing behavior/disciplinary problems, because academic or behavior problems might be a symptom of psychiatric challenges or emotional distress.

REFERENCES

Adams, C. J., Robelen, E. W., & Shah, N. (2012). Data show retention disparities. *Education Week, 31*(23), 1.

Andrews, G., & Peters, L. (1998). The psychometric properties of the composite international diagnostic interview. *Social Psychiatry and Psychiatric Epidemiology, 33*(2), 80–88.

Ansary, N. S., & Luthar, S. S. (2009). Distress and academic achievement among adolescents of affluence: A study of externalizing and internalizing problem behaviors and school performance. *Development and Psychopathology, 21*(1), 319–341.

Aud, S., Fox, M., & Kewal Ramani, A. (2010). *Status and trends in the education of racial and ethnic groups* (NCES 2010-015). U.S. Department of Education, National Center for Education Statistics. Washington, DC: U.S. Government Printing Office.

Basch, C. E. (2011). Healthier students are better learners: A missing link in school reforms to close the achievement gap. *Journal of School Health, 81*(10), 593–598.

Bradshaw, C. P., Sawyer, A. L., & O'Brennan, L. M. (2009). A social disorganization perspective on bullying-related attitudes and behaviors: The influence of school context. *Journal of Community Psychology, 43*, 204–220.

Bradshaw, C. P., Waasdorp, T. E., Goldweber, A., & Johnson, S. L. (2013). Bullies, gangs, drugs, and school: Understanding the overlap and the role of ethnicity and urbanicity. *Journal of Youth and Adolescence, 42*(2), 220–234. doi: 10.1007 /s10964-012-9863-7

Brady, S. S., Winston, W., & Gockley, S. E. (2014). Stress-related externalizing behavior among African American youth: How could policy and practice transform risk into resilience? *Journal of Social Issues, 70*(2), 315–341.

Ceballo, R., McLoyd, V. C., & Toyokawa, T. (2004). The influence of neighborhood quality on adolescents' educational values and school effort. *Journal of Adolescent Research, 19*(6), 716–739.

Chen, K. W., Killeya-Jones, L. A., & Vega, W (2005). Prevalence and co-occurrence of psychiatric symptom clusters in the U.S. adolescent population using DISC predicative scales. *Clinical Practice and Epidemiology in Mental Health, 1*, 1–12. doi:10.1186/1745-0179-1-22

Clayton, J. K. (2011). Changing diversity in U.S. schools: The impact on elementary student performance and achievement. *Education and Urban Society, 43*(6), 671–695.

Davis, J. E., & Jordan, W. J. (1994). The effects of school context, structure and experiences on African American males in middle and high school. *Journal of Negro Education, 63*(4), 570–587.

Dubow, E. F., Huesmann, R. L., Boxer, P., Pulkkinen, L., & Kokko, K. (2006). Middle childhood and adolescent contextual and personal predictors of adult educational and occupational outcomes: A mediational model in two countries. *Developmental Psychology, 42*(5), 937–949.

Gibbs, J. T. (1990). Mental health issues of black adolescents: Implications for policy and practice. In A. Stiffman & L. Davis (Eds.), *Ethnic issues in adolescent mental health* (pp. 21–52). Newbury Park: CA: Sage.

Greene, M. B. (2005). Reducing violence and aggression in schools. *Trauma, Violence, & Abuse, 6*(3), 236–253.

Jackson, J. S., Torres, M., Caldwell, C. H., Neighbors, H. W., Nesse, R. M., Taylor, R. J., ... Williams, D. R. (2004). The national survey of American life: A study of racial, ethnic and cultural influences on mental disorders and mental health. *International Journal of Methods in Psychiatric Research, 13*(4), 196–207.

Jacob, B. A. (2007). The challenges of staffing urban schools with effective teachers. *The Future of Children, 17*(1), 129–153.

Joe, S., Baser, R. S., Neighbors, H. W., Caldwell, C. H., & Jackson, J. S. (2009). 12-month and lifetime prevalence of suicide attempts among black adolescents in the national survey of American life. *Journal of the American Academy of Child & Adolescent Psychiatry, 48*(3), 271–283.

Kessler, R. C., Avenevoli, S., Costello, J., Georgiades, K., Green, J. G., Gruber, M. J., ... Merikangas, K. M. (2012). Prevalence, persistence, and sociodemographic correlates of DSM-IV disorders in the national comorbidity survey replication adolescent supplement. *Archives of General Psychiatry, 69,* 372–380. doi:10.1001/arch genpsychiatry.2011.160

Kessler, R. C., & Ustun, T. B. (2004). The World Mental Health (WMH) Survey Initiative version of the World Health Organization (WHO) Composite International Diagnostic Interview (CIDI). *International Journal of Methods in Psychiatric Research, 13*(2), 93–121.

Lambert, S., Herman, K., Bynum, M., & Ialongo, N. (2009). Perceptions of racism and depressive symptoms in African American adolescents: The role of perceived academic and social control. *Journal of Youth & Adolescence, 38*(4), 519–531. doi: 10.1007/s10964-009-9393-0

Levin, B. (2009). Enduring issues in urban education. *Journal of Comparative Policy Analysis, 11*(2), 181–195.

McLaughlin, K. A., Breslau, J., Green J. G., Lakoma, M. D., Sampson, N. A., Zaslavsky, A. M., & Kessler, R. C. (2011). Childhood socio-economic status and the onset, persistence, and severity of DSM-IV mental disorders in a US national sample. *Social Science & Medicine, 73*(7), 1088–1096.

McLeod, J. D., & Fettes, D. L. (2007). Trajectories of failure: The educational careers of children with mental health problems. *American Journal of Sociology, 113*(3), 653–701.

Myers, H. F. (1989). Urban stress and mental health in black youth: An epidemiologic and conceptual update. In R. L. Jones (Ed.), *Black adolescents* (pp. 123–152). Berkeley, CA: Cobb & Henry.

Nagin, D. S., Pagani, L., Tremblay, R. E., & Vitaro, F. (2003). Life course turning points: The effect of grade retention on physical aggression. *Development and Psychopathology, 15*(2), 343–361.

Noguera, P. A. (2003). The trouble with Black boys: The role and influence of environmental and cultural factors on the academic performance of African American males. *Urban Education, 38*(4), 431–459.

Orfield, G., & Lee, C. (2005). *Why segregation matters: Poverty and educational inequality.* Retrieved from http://civilrightsproject.ucla.edu/research/k-12-educa tion/integration-and-diversity/why-segregation-matters-poverty-and-educational -inequality/orfield-why-segregation-matters-2005.pdf

Peterson, A., & Hamburg, B. (1986). Adolescence: A developmental approach to problems and psychopathology. *Behavior Therapy, 17,* 480–499.

Rose, T., Joe, S., Shields, J., & Caldwell, C. H. (2014). Social integration and the mental health of Black adolescents. *Child Development, 85*(3), 1003–1018. doi: 10.1111 /cdev.12182

Rosella, J. D., & Albrecht, S. A. (1993). Toward an understanding of the health status of black adolescents: An application of the stress-coping framework. *Issues in Comprehensive Pediatric Nursing, 16*(4), 193–205.

Rothon, C., Head, J., Klineberg, E., & Stansfeld, S. (2011). Can social support protect bullied adolescents from adverse outcomes? A prospective study on the effects of bullying on the educational achievement and mental health of adolescents at secondary schools in East London. *Journal of Adolescence, 34*(3), 579–588. doi:10.1016/j.adolescence.2010.02.007

Rowling, L. (2006). Adolescence and emerging adulthood (12–17 years and 18–24 years). In M. Cattan & S. Tilford (Eds.), *Mental health promotion: A lifespan approach* (pp. 100–136). Maidenhead, England: Open University Press.

Ryan, A. M. (2000). Peer groups as a context for the socialization of adolescents' motivation, engagement, and achievement in school. *Educational Psychologist, 35*(2), 101–111.

Serbin, L. A., Temcheff, C. E., Cooperman, J. M., Stack, D. M., Ledingham, J., & Schwartzman, A. E. (2011). Predicting family poverty and other disadvantaged conditions for child rearing from childhood aggression and social withdrawal: A 30-year longitudinal study. *International Journal of Behavioral Development, 35*(2), 97–106.

Sweetman, J., Baser, R., Faison, K., Rafferty, J., Torres, M., & Matusko, N. (2009). *The national survey of American life: Methods and analysis.* Unpublished manuscript.

Thompson, T., Jr., & Massat, C. R. (2005). Experiences of violence, post-traumatic stress, academic achievement and behavior problems of urban African-American children. *Child and Adolescent Social Work Journal, 22*(5–6), 367–393.

U.S. Department of Health and Human Services. (2001). *Mental health: Culture, race, and ethnicity—A supplement to mental health: A report of the surgeon general.* Rockville, MD: U.S. Department of Health and Human Services, Substance Abuse and Mental Health Services Administration, Center for Mental Health Services, National Institutes of Health, National Institute of Mental Health. Retrieved from http://www.surgeongeneral.gov/library/mentalhealth/cre/

Weist, D. J., Wong, E. H., & Kreil, D. A. (1998). Predictors of global self-worth and academic performance among regular education, learning disabled, and continuation high school students. *Adolescence, 33*(131), 601–618.

Whaley, A. L., & Noel, L. T. (2013). Academic achievement and behavioral health among Asian American and African American adolescents: Testing the model minority and inferior minority assumptions. *Social Psychology of Education, 16*(1), 23–43. doi:10.1007/s11218-012-9206-2

5 Community violence, adolescent aggression, and academic achievement

Nadine M. Finigan-Carr
and Tanya L. Sharpe

Community violence exposure is the "chronic and pervasive presence of violence and violence-related events within an individual's proximal environment" (Jipguep & Sanders-Phillips, 2003, p. 380). In the United States, the neighborhoods most affected by community violence are also those most affected by poverty with a high concentration of underrepresented minorities in urban environments (Beyers, Loeber, Per-Olof, & Stouthamer-Loeber, 2001; Copeland-Linder et al., 2007). In addition, children and young adults ages 12 to 24 appear to be the majority of individuals who suffer more violent crime than any other age group in these urban environments (Warner & Swisher, 2014). Youth not only experience violence in the roles of victim or perpetrator, they also are harmed by being witnesses to community violence. The National Longitudinal Study of Adolescent Health (Resnick, Ireland, & Borowsky, 2004) found that over 1 in 10 middle- and high-school youth witness a shooting or stabbing each year. Among African American youth, nearly 1 in 4 had this experience, and experiencing chronic forms of community violence has its consequences. Community violence is negatively related to school performance, having an effect on both long-term outcomes such as grade point average and proximal outcomes such as school engagement. African American youth who are disproportionately exposed to community violence have an increased risk for emotional and behavioral symptoms that can detract from learning and undermine academic achievement (Busby, Lambert, & Ialongo, 2013).

In rural communities and urban neighborhoods across the United States, the issue of youth violence has become endemic. This is especially true in communities that are largely African American, characterized by concentrated poverty, and, as a result, have limited structural resources. As a result, African American youth are most vulnerable to injury or death due to violence or violent-related causes. Research on youth violence has examined adolescent aggression as a predictor of violent behaviors (Roberto, Meyer, Boster, & Roberto, 2003). Aggression has been defined as behaviors that are intended to hurt or harm others, including verbal and physical behaviors that cause either psychological or bodily harm (Orpinas & Frankowski, 2001).

Aggressive behaviors in youth are complex with antecedents in childhood experiences, community norms, and social and economic conditions.

Ethnic minority youth, in this case African Americans, tend to grow up in ecological niches,[1] which, in many cases, hinder rather than promote successful development. This ecological niche can influence both an individual's inherent propensities for aggression, as well as provide opportunities for aggression to be learned over time (Guerra & Williams, 2006). The niche can provide a wide context for adolescents' development, which includes immediate sources of social influence (peers, family, and neighbors) situated within a greater societal context.

In neighborhoods characterized by concentrated poverty and high levels of community violence, African American adolescents' ecological niche may promote rather than prohibit aggressive behaviors. In examination of adolescent development within this niche, one should consider the immediate sources of social influence within the context of education and the overall neighborhood environment. These societal contexts represent social determinants of health, which have an impact not just on aggressive behavior, but on overall well-being.

SOCIAL MILIEU OF NEIGHBORHOODS CHARACTERIZED BY HIGH LEVELS OF COMMUNITY VIOLENCE

Despite considerable attention from researchers, community-based organizations, policy makers, and law enforcement, community violence persists as a major public health problem in the United States (Voisin, 2007). Neighborhoods characterized by poverty, prevalent substance abuse, inadequate income, densely populated urban areas, low educational attainment of caregivers, high rates of unemployment, and poor environmental conditions are linked to communities that experience high rates of violent crime (Bradshaw, Waasdorp, Goldweber, & Johnson, 2013; Tolan, Sherrod, Gorman-Smith, & Henry, 2004). Violence at the individual and community levels have been linked to deficits in institutional resources, collective efficacy, and community cohesion (Sampson, Morenoff, & Gannon-Rowley, 2002; Sampson & Raudenbush, 1997). In addition to neighborhood structural characteristics, firearm availability and ethnic heterogeneity appear correlated with increased rates of violence (Bradshaw et al., 2013; Sampson & Raudenbush, 1997).

Research on community violence, adolescent aggression, and academic achievement has typically focused on the correlation between mediating variables, such as socioeconomic status (SES), social capital, violent exposure, and their impact on moderator outcomes such as aggressive behavior,

---

1   An ecological niche refers to the sociospatial locations where specific groups of people reside (Guerra & Williams, 2006).

academic performance, and achievement (Chen, Voisin, & Jacobson, 2013; Lambert, Boyd, Cammack, & Ialongo, 2012; McDonald, Deatrick, Kassam-Adams, & Richmond, 2011; Stoddard, Henly, Sieving, & Bolland, 2011). The outcomes of these studies often conclude that aggressive behavior has been found to mediate the association between community violence exposure and academic performance for both African American males and females (Busby et al., 2013). However, lost in these examinations is the social cultural context in which community violence and academic achievement is perceived and achieved. Researchers, such as McNulty and Bellair (2003) and Mouw (2000), support the inclusion of larger structural factors (e.g., concentrated poverty, structural racism) in the examination of community violence, adolescent aggression, and developmental and behavioral outcomes. The characterization of neighborhoods that experience high rates of violent crime based solely on demographic characteristics (e.g., SES, educational attainment) risks the politicization of community members, the majority of whom are African American and Latino in a pejorative manner.

THE LINK BETWEEN EDUCATION AND AGGRESSION

Educational experiences serve as antecedents to African American adolescents' success later in life. Therefore, educational inequities have the potential for broad consequences on their future educational attainment, employment, and relationships. The evidence points to unique academic challenges faced by African American students who exhibit aggressive behaviors in school contexts. Reductions in aggression would be of value to schools because, in addition to the intrinsic worth of preventing violence, these effects would strengthen the educational process (Shapiro, Burgoon, Welker, & Clough, 2002). When verbal or physical aggression occurs in the school setting, it can disrupt classrooms, distract students from their work, and divert school staff from teaching. The ecological niche in which African American youth develop has been seen as an unsafe environment leading to increased aggressive behaviors, decreased school engagement, and low proficiency in school.

Many linkages have been found in the extant research between aggression and academic achievement. Academic achievement is largely the product of ability and previous academic history. As aggressive behaviors are highly and disproportionately prevalent among African American youth, they have a negative impact on academic achievement by adversely affecting cognition, school connectedness, and absenteeism. Aggressive youth have been found to spend more time in fights and arguments, in detention or suspension, and avoiding school; thereby spending less time on academic work and learning (Basch, 2011). More specifically, schools tend to rely heavily on exclusion of African American students from the classroom as a disciplinary strategy in response to aggressive behaviors thereby exacerbating racial gaps in academic achievement (Davis & Jordan, 1994; Gregory, Skiba, & Noguera, 2010). Students who display aggressive behaviors develop patterns of low academic achievement and performance (Miles & Stipek, 2006).

Academic engagement is one aspect of motivation for achievement and is comprised of three dimensions: participation, identification, and school expectations (Sirin & Rogers-Sirin, 2005). *Participation* is the behavioral dimension, which refers to activities such as attending class on time and participating in class discussions. *Identification* refers to affective aspects of school engagement, such as whether the students' feel as if they belong in school or identify with people in the school environment. The third dimension, *school expectations*, emerges from adolescent development research and refers to students' desire to continue in school and beliefs about their potential to attend college. Academic engagement increases the potential for educational success and is inconsistent with antisocial behavior, such as aggression.

Research examining the link between aggression and engagement has shown that adolescents' aggressive behaviors directly affect their academic engagement and ability to learn (Miles & Stipek, 2006). African American youth from impoverished environments—both urban and rural—exhibit increased academic engagement when their school contexts provide structure and support. Concurrently, these engaged students will suppress aggressive behaviors, as these would interfere with learning by participation and result in them losing their connection to school (Irvin, 2012). African American youth who are known to be aggressive have frequent encounters with authority figures resulting in disciplinary actions, which are perceived as unfair. As the situation is perceived as hostile, aggressive youth tend to no longer identify with the school environment resulting in disengagement with an impact on their grade point average (Graham, Bellmore, & Mize, 2006). This is in line with social learning theories, which propose that youth's interpersonal relationships and ties to conventional institutions that value law-abiding behaviors can decrease their likelihood of engaging in delinquent behaviors and activities. However, neighborhoods that are characterized as dangerous and violent can limit youth's opportunities to be involved in organizations that foster law-abiding behaviors.

COMMUNITY VIOLENCE, ADOLESCENT AGGRESSION, AND ACADEMIC ACHIEVEMENT: A THEORETICAL PERSPECTIVE

Examining the social cultural context in which community violence, adolescent aggression, and academic achievement occurs requires an examination of both perceptions and beliefs regarding the causes and experiences with community violence; and, institutional structures that dictate the distribution of goods and services (e.g., education, employment, housing, mental health care) that adolescents ultimately need to cope as a result of being exposed to chronic forms of community violence. Therefore, we must begin to use macrolevel theories that push us beyond the examination of interpersonal relationships and behavior toward the inclusion of the role of institutional structures and policies that perpetuate and therefore contribute to the systemic and cyclical nature of community violence, adolescent aggression, and academic achievement.

To generate evidence relevant to the role of institutional structures and policies that influence adolescent aggression and academic achievement and interventions that are developed to address it, the following theoretical approaches are offered. Sharpe (2015) offers a Model of Coping for African American Survivors of Homicide Victims (MCAASHV) that illustrates the sociocultural lens by which African American survivors of homicide victims appraise the impact of experiencing the homicide of a loved one and assess available and approachable resources to cope with it. This model is particularly relevant to the examination of community violence, adolescent aggression, and academic achievement in two very distinct ways. First, African American adolescents living in areas plagued by systemic poverty are disproportionately exposed to this specific form of community violence as homicide is the leading cause of death among African American youth aged 15 to 24 (Laurie & Neimeyer, 2008). Second, the MCAASHV (Sharpe, 2015), solicits a macrolevel examination to coping with homicide violence and victimization by considering the manner in which experiencing the homicide of a loved one is appraised and the impact that the appraisal has on coping resources and strategies.

For African Americans, experiencing the traumatic stressful event of homicide does not simply call for an appraisal of the stressful event to determine what type of coping strategies are available for use to preserve one's well-being. Rather, African Americans racially appraise the impact of experiencing a homicide through systems that place value on the experience of homicide and bring about feelings of stigma, blame, and a lack of justice. Simultaneously African Americans are confronted with historical cultural trauma that is experienced by being an African American existing in a racist society. McGuffey (2013) refers to this appraisal as racial appraisal.

Racial appraisal suggests that both culture (a system of beliefs) and structure (a societal pattern that dictates the distribution of resources "unevenly" throughout the United States for communities of color) must be considered in the examination of disenfranchised populations of color's perception, availability, and utilization of coping resources (McGuffey, 2013). Therefore, for populations of color who experience trauma, the experience of the traumatic event is not simply appraised; rather it is "racially appraised" for the purpose of determining resources that are readily available to assist individuals in coping with traumatic experiences. Racial appraisal exposes how cultural trauma influences perceptions and expectations of mental health resources, social services, distributive justice, and so on based on racial status and race-based structural inequality. Race-based structural inequality inevitably influences the interpretation of homicide and impacts African American survivors' coping responses to it.

School engagement is one of the many ways adolescents receive support and thrive both academically and socially (Brackett, Reyes, Rivers, Elbertson, & Salovey, 2011; Brock, Nishida, Chiong, Grimm, & Rimm-Kaufman, 2008). In fact, it has been well documented that schools often serve as a protective factor to coping with a myriad of stressful experiences including community violence. Conversely, exposure to community violence negatively impacts academic performance and achievement. Now if schools are the primary domain in which adolescents perform and are thereby assessed (Borofsky, Kellerman, Baucom, Oliver, & Margolin, 2013), and the structure of that domain and dissemination of its knowledge is subject to race-based structural inequality, are we accurately examining the causes and consequences of community violence, adolescent aggression, and academic achievement? Are we not conducting research, informing policy, and developing interventions from a masked racialized lens that ignores the impact of racism on communities that chronically experience violence and victimization and are disproportionately African American? The MCAASHV (Sharpe, 2015) provides a foundation by which historical and contemporary experiences of racial identity development is considered in the examination of the African American experience of coping with violent traumatic experiences.

The MCAASHV (Sharpe, 2015) asks us to consider the psychosocial, cultural, and structural process of adaptation that African American adolescents must venture through in order to "survive" violent experiences. The adolescents' experiences are subjectively based on their perception and experiences that are shaped by both cultural beliefs and unequal societal structures that impact the utilization and allocation of psychosocial coping resources. Thus, if cultural and structurally responsive resources are perceived as unavailable, alternatives to coping with violent victimization can result in compromised academic achievement and aggression.

BUILDING PARENT–SCHOOL PARTNERSHIPS FOR STUDENT SUCCESS

When African American students are exposed to community violence and other environmental stressors, including trauma, it impedes their ability to meet academic benchmarks (Cooley-Strickland et al., 2009). Exposure to trauma has been reported as a barrier to nonviolent behavior leading to increased adolescent aggression (Farrell, Henry, Schoeny, Bettencourt, & Tolan, 2010). However, when proximal support, supervision, and/or monitoring occur within the neighborhood, nonviolent behaviors may increase. Considering that one of the best sources of support, supervision, and monitoring comes from parent involvement, schools should consider building strong parent–school partnerships at all academic levels in order to ensure students' academic success.

Parents overwhelmingly want the best for their children. They consistently feel that they have a role in their child's education and are interested in being involved in their child's education at home and at school (Murray et al., 2014). In neighborhoods characterized by community violence, parents report negative and sometimes hostile interactions with teachers and other school staff, which can present as a barrier to parent involvement (Barton, Drake, Perez, & St. Louis, 2004; Koonce & Harper, 2005). African American parents may also perceive racism in their interactions with the schools as well (Kim, 2009; Koonce & Harper, 2005; Van Velsor & Orozco, 2007). Parents have indicated that even in the absence of school-based barriers, there are various scheduling issues that present a challenge to school involvement, including work, raising children, and other family responsibilities (e.g., preparing meals, serving as caregiver for elderly relatives) (Murray et al., 2014). This is especially relevant to parents in single-headed households or of lower socioeconomic status (Van Velsor & Orozco, 2007).

For schools to build stronger parent–school partnerships, an understanding of these barriers is necessary in order for them to make practical changes, which will enhance parent involvement. This can start with tailoring school-based parent involvement activities to address the barriers experienced by parents' personal life context. For example, schools can implement more reliable and timely methods of communication, schedule school meetings and events at varied or multiple times to work around family schedules, and solicit parents' ideas on other ways to overcome scheduling barriers. In addition, school counselors, social workers, and other human services professionals can help to foster positive parent–teacher relationships. This can be done in two distinct ways. First, they can educate teachers on how best to work with parents and on their motivational beliefs, and how to best provide opportunities for involvement both at home and at school. Second, they can encourage parent visits by greeting and orienting them to potential school-based, parent-involvement opportunities, thereby boosting the positive aspects of the school climate. In so doing, schools can become a place that promote community building and shared goals leading to improved child well-being.

CONCLUSION

The impact of structural inequality that impacts educational opportunity and influences neighborhood disadvantage is especially profound during childhood and adolescence. As schools in underserved communities have fewer resources, they are not always equipped to provide comprehensive services to students who are traumatically victimized by chronic forms of community violence. Considering how trauma affects mental health and physical well-being throughout the lifespan, it is important to consider models such as the

MCAASHV that consider the social and cultural context of coping with community violence when identifying and developing interventions designed to increase student aggression and increase academic engagement for the overall school success of African American youth. In addition, family support in the form of parent involvement should be encouraged via strong parent–school partnerships in order to decrease student engagement in aggressive behavior. Ensuring healthy development requires reducing children's exposure to neighborhood stressors and nurturing family caregiving functioning.

REFERENCES

Barton, A. C., Drake, C., Perez, J. G., & St. Louis, K. (2004). Ecologies of parental engagement in urban education. *Educational Researcher, 33*(4), 3–13.

Basch, C. E. (2011). Aggression and violence and the achievement gap among urban minority youth. *Journal of School Health, 81*(10), 619–625. doi:10.1111 /j.1746-1561.2011.00636.x

Beyers, J., Loeber, R., Per-Olof, H., & Stouthamer-Loeber, M. (2001). What predicts adolescent violence in better-off neighborhoods? *Journal of Abnormal Child Psychology, 29*(5), 369–381.

Borofsky, L. A., Kellerman, I., Baucom, B., Oliver, P. H., & Margolin, G. (2013). Community violence exposure and adolescents' school engagement and academic achievement over time. *Psychology of Violence, 3*(4), 381–395.

Brackett, M. A., Reyes, M. R., Rivers, S. E., Elbertson, N. A., & Salovey, P. (2011). Classroom emotional climate, teacher affiliation, and student conduct. *The Journal of Classroom Interaction, 46*, 27–36.

Bradshaw, C. P., Waasdorp, T. E., Goldweber, A., & Johnson, S. L. (2013). Bullies, gangs, drugs, and school: Understanding the overlap and the role of ethnicity and urbanicity. *Journal of Youth and Adolescence, 42*(2), 220–234. doi:10.1007 /s10964-012-9863-7

Brock, L. L., Nishida, T. K., Chiong, C., Grimm, K. J., & Rimm-Kaufman, S. E. (2008). Children's perceptions of the classroom environment and social and academic performance: A longitudinal analysis of the contribution of the Responsive Classroom approach. *Journal of School Psychology, 46*(2), 129–149.

Busby, D. R., Lambert, S. F., & Ialongo, N. S. (2013). Psychological symptoms linking exposure to community violence and academic functioning in African American adolescents. *Journal of Youth and Adolescence*. doi:10.1007/s10964-012-9895-z

Chen, P., Voisin, D. R., & Jacobson, K. C. (2013). Community violence exposure and adolescent delinquency: Examining a spectrum of promotive factors. *Youth & Society*. doi:10.1177/ 0044118X13475827

Cooley-Strickland, M., Quille, T. J., Griffin, R. S., Stuart, E. A., Bradshaw, C. P., & Furr-Holden, D. (2009). Community violence and youth: Affect, behavior, substance use, and academics. *Clinical Child & Family Psychology Review, 12*(2), 127–156. doi:10.1007/s10567-009-0051-6

Copeland-Linder, N., Jones, V., Haynie, D., Simons-Morton, B., Wright, J., & Cheng, T. (2007). Factors associated with retaliatory attitudes among African-American adolescents who have been assaulted. *Journal of Pediatric Psychology, 32*(7), 760–770. doi:10.1093/jpepsy/jsm007

Davis, J. E., & Jordan, W. J. (1994). The effects of school context, structure and experiences on African American males in middle and high school. *Journal of Negro Education, 63*(4), 570–587.

Farrell, A. D., Henry, D. B., Schoeny, M. E., Bettencourt, A., & Tolan, R. H. (2010). Normative beliefs and self-efficacy for nonviolence as moderators of peer, school, and parental risk factors for aggression in early adolescence. *Journal of Clinical Child and Adolescent Psychology, 39*(6), 800–813.

Graham, S., Bellmore, A. D., & Mize, J. (2006). Peer victimization, aggression and their co-occurrence in middle school: Pathways to adjustment problems. *Journal of Abnormal Child Psychology, 34*(3), 363–378. doi:10.1007/s10802-006-9030-2

Gregory, A., Skiba, R. J., & Noguera, P. A. (2010). The achievement gap and the discipline gap: Two sides of the same coin? *Educational Researcher, 39*(1), 59–68. doi:10.3102/0013189x09357621

Guerra, N. G., & Williams, K. R. (2006). Ethnicity, youth violence and the etiology of development. In N. G. Guerra & E. P. Smith (Eds.), *Preventing youth violence in a multicultural society* (pp. 17–45). Washington, DC: American Psychological Association.

Irvin, M. J. (2012). Role of student engagement in the resilience of African American adolescents from low-income rural communities. *Psychology in the Schools, 49*(2), 176–193.

Jipguep, M. C., & Sanders-Phillips, K. (2003). The context of violence for children of color: Violence in the community and in the media. *Journal of Negro Education, 72*(4), 379–395.

Kim, Y. (2009). Minority parental involvement and school barriers: Moving the focus away from deficiencies of parents. *Educational Research Review, 4*(2), 80–102. doi:10.1016/j.edurev.2009.02.003

Koonce, D. A., & Harper, W. (2005). Engaging African American parents in the schools: A community-based consultation model. *Journal of Educational and Psychological Consultation, 16*(1 & 2), 55–74.

Lambert, S. F., Boyd, R. C., Cammack, N. L., & Ialongo, N. S. (2012). Relationship proximity to victims of witnessed community violence: Associations with adolescent internalizing and externalizing behaviors. *American Journal of Orthopsychiatry, 82*(1), 1–9. doi:http://dx.doi.org/10.1111/j.1939-0025.2011.01135.x

Laurie, A., & Neimeyer, R. A. (2008). African Americans in bereavement: Grief as a function of ethnicity. *Omega-Journal of Death and Dying, 57*(2), 173–193.

McDonald, C. C., Deatrick, J. A., Kassam-Adams, N., & Richmond, T. S. (2011). Community violence exposure and positive youth development in urban youth. *Journal of Community Health, 36*(6), 925–932.

McGuffey, C. S. (2013). Rape and racial appraisals. *Du Bois Review: Social Science Research on Race, 10*(1), 109–130.

McNulty, T. L., & Bellair, P. E. (2003). Explaining racial and ethnic differences in serious adolescent violent behavior. *Criminology, 41*(3), 709–747.

Miles, S. B., & Stipek, D. (2006). Contemporaneous and longitudinal associations between social behvior and literacy achievement in a sample of low-income elementary school children. *Child Development, 77*, 103–117.

Mouw, T. (2000). Job relocation and the racial gap in unemployment in Detroit and Chicago, 1980 to 1990. *American Sociological Review, 65*(5), 730–753.

Murray, K. W., Finigan-Carr, N., Jones, V., Copeland-Linder, N., Haynie, D. L., & Cheng, T. L. (2014). Barriers and facilitators to school-based parent involvement for parents of urban public middle school students. *SAGE Open, 4*(4). doi:10.1177/2158244014558030

Orpinas, P., & Frankowski, R. (2001). The aggression scale: A self-report measure of aggressive behavior in young adults. *Journal of Early Adolescents, 21*, 50–67.

Resnick, M. D., Ireland, M., & Borowsky, I. (2004). Youth violence perpetration: What protects? What predicts? Findings from the National Longitudinal Study of Adolescent Health. *Journal of Adolescent Health, 35*, 424.e1–424.e10.

Roberto, A., Meyer, G., Boster, F., & Roberto, H. (2003). Adolescents' decisions about verbal and physical aggression: An application of the theory of reasoned action. *Human Communication Research, 29*(1), 135–147.

Sampson, R., Morenoff, J., & Gannon-Rowley, T. (2002). Assessing "neighborhood effects": Social processes and new directions in research. *Annual Review of Sociology, 28*, 443–478.

Sampson, R., & Raudenbush, S. (1997). Neighborhoods and violent crime: A multilevel study of collective efficacy. *Science, 277*(5328), 918–924.

Shapiro, J. P., Burgoon, J. D., Welker, C. J., & Clough, J. B. (2002). Evaluation of The Peacemakers Program: School-based violence prevention for students in grades four through eight. *Psychology in the Schools, 39*(1), 87–100.

Sharpe, T. L. (2015). Understanding the sociocultural context of coping for African American family members of homicide victims: A conceptual model. *Trauma, Violence, & Abuse, 16*(1), 48–59.

Sirin, S. R., & Rogers-Sirin, L. (2005). Components of school engagement among African American adolescents. *Applied Developmental Science, 9*(1), 5–13. doi:10.1207/s1532480xads0901_2

Stoddard, S. A., Henly, S. J., Sieving, R. E., & Bolland, J. (2011). Social connections, trajectories of hopelessness, and serious violence in impoverished urban youth. *Journal of Youth and Adolescence, 40*(3), 278–295. doi:http://dx.doi.org/10.1007/s10964-010-9580-z

Tolan, P. H., Sherrod, L. R., Gorman-Smith, D., & Henry, D. B. (2004). Building protection, support, and opportunity for inner-city children and youth and their families. In K. I. Maton, C. J. Schellenbach, B. J. Leadbeter, & A. L. Solarz (Eds.), *Investing in children, youth, families and communities: Strengths-based research and policy* (pp. 193–211). Washington, DC: American Psychological Association.

Van Velsor, P., & Orozco, G. (2007). Involving low income parents in the schools: Communitycentric strategies for school counselors. *Professional School Counseling, 11*(1), 17–24.

Voisin, D. R. (2007). The effects of family and community violence exposure among youth: Recommendations for practice and policy. *Journal of Social Work Education, 43*, 51–66.

Warner, T. D., & Swisher, R. R. (2014). The effect of direct and indirect exposure to violence on youth survival expectations. *Journal of Adolescent Health, 55*(6), 817–822.

Part II

Interventions with an impact on both health behaviors and educational outcomes

6 Schools as retraumatizing environments

Wendy E. Shaia and Shanda C. Crowder

Many African American children in urban environments arrive at school experiencing the effects of complex trauma from their homes and communities, only to find that schools are environments where their trauma goes unrecognized and may be inadvertently exacerbated. In some school settings, the entire school community is exposed to trauma through a variety of events on a daily basis. In other cases, children experience new trauma in schools, as school staff attempt to discipline children for what they believe to be inappropriate behavior, as opposed to responses to the effects of trauma. Often, African American children experience more punitive consequences than do their peers of other races for the same behavior. This chapter will provide case examples of how children and school communities are retraumatized in schools, provide the context for their trauma, and offer potential solutions, using a trauma-informed perspective.

CHILDHOOD TRAUMA IN THE URBAN ENVIRONMENT

Many children in urban environments, particularly when those urban environments are poor, are exposed to adverse experiences, which may also be traumatic. The National Child Traumatic Stress Network (NCTSN) defines childhood trauma as a child having (1) experienced a serious injury him- or herself or having witnessed a serious injury to or the death of someone else; or (2) faced imminent threats of serious injury or death to him or herself or others; or (3) experienced a violation of personal physical integrity. Child traumatic stress occurs when children are overwhelmed by their experiences of traumatic events or situations, and when that sense of being overwhelmed impacts their ability to cope with their day-to-day lives (National Child Traumatic Stress Network, 2015). Not every child who experiences traumatic events or experiences also experiences childhood traumatic stress.

Adverse childhood experiences (ACEs) may impact children into adulthood, and include verbal, physical, or sexual abuse, as well as many types of household/family dysfunction, such as having a family member who is in prison, mentally ill, substance abusing, absent from separation or divorce, or experiencing domestic violence (Centers for Disease Control, 2010). A survey of over 8,000 individuals conducted by a large HMO asked about ACEs and health outcomes. This study found a relationship between the exposure to ACEs and disease, including some of the leading causes of death as adults. The prevalence and risk increased for smoking, severe obesity, depression, and suicide attempts as number of childhood exposure to ACEs increased. Additionally, although there were a relatively small number of African American participants in the study, these participants reported a higher number of two, three, and four ACEs than White participants (Felitti et al., 1998). A later study by Finkelhor, Shattuck, Turner, and Hamby (2015) concluded that additional factors, such as exposure to community violence and low socioeconomic status (SES) are also important predictors of physical and mental health problems, although low SES alone was a predictor of health status, but not significant in predicting psychological distress.

It is becoming increasingly clear to researchers, child health practitioners, and social service workers that many children and youth are exposed to violence at staggering rates in their homes and communities. In a national sample of families, 60% of children and youth reported having experienced or witnessed victimization of some type in the previous year; almost half had experienced physical assault, 10% some type of child maltreatment, 6% sexual victimization, and a quarter had witnessed or experienced some other type of indirect victimization, including 10% witnessing assault within their own families. More than one-third had experienced two or more direct victimizations, more than 10% had five or more, 2% had 10 or more (Finkelhor, Turner, Ormrod, & Hamby, 2009). Other studies have found that up to 90% of children in some environments have been exposed to family and/or community violence (Crusto et al., 2010; Slep & O'Leary, 2005).

Beginning in the 1970s and 1980s, urban communities saw a dramatic increase in concentrated urban poverty, as racial housing restrictions in the suburbs eased, and upwardly mobile African Americans moved into the suburbs, leaving behind a concentration of very poor families and individuals. Other theories about elements contributing to the increased concentration of poverty in urban communities include the loss of manufacturing and other local jobs, economic and social disinvestment in cities, blight, and decay (Sessoms & Wolch, 2008; Yang & Jargowsky, 2006). Additionally, African American and Hispanic children are much more likely to live in poverty than their White counterparts, and those African American or Hispanic children are overwhelmingly more likely to live in communities made up mostly by people of the same race (Drake & Rank, 2009). This concentration of poverty is seen most clearly in older, industrial cities in the Northeast, such as Newark, New York, and Baltimore (Ricketts & Sawhill, 1988).

While concentrations of poverty decreased in the 1990s, these Northeast cities still see a significant concentration of very poor people living in certain neighborhoods. In fact, urban poverty should consistently be considered within the neighborhood context, even more than in the family context since, even if a particular family is not impoverished, that family will experience a number of significant disadvantages, and the children will be exposed to the cumulative effects of multiple risk factors, simply by virtue of living in a neighborhood with concentrated poverty (Drake & Rank, 2009).

In some urban settings, children may be exposed to the cumulative effects of multiple risk factors, including the effects of poverty, maltreatment, violence, and parental stress, which often coexist (Appleyard, Egeland, VanDulmen, & Sroufe, 2005; Wadsworth & Santiago, 2008). Children, as young as preschoolers, often carry the weight of poverty-related stress, either because they are directly impacted by food insufficiency and inadequate housing, or because they are cared for by frustrated, irritable, worried parents (Ackerman & Izard, 1999; McLoyd, 1990; Wadsworth & Berger, 2006; Wadsworth & Santiago, 2008).

According to the National Child Traumatic Stress Network (2015), children experiencing traumatic stress often have difficulty regulating their emotions and/or behavior, and may be easily frightened, clingy, fearful, and/or aggressive and impulsive. Other symptoms include being withdrawn, difficulty concentrating, having memory problems, excessive anger or acting out, physical symptoms like headaches and stomach aches, difficulty trusting others, and demanding attention through both positive and negative behaviors. Children may also experience appetite or digestive issues, difficulty sleeping, or bedwetting. Many of these symptoms are evident for children at home, out in their communities, and at school.

THE IMPACT OF TRAUMA ON BRAIN DEVELOPMENT

Childhood is a critical time for brain development, and determines how the child will progress through adolescence and into adulthood. The human brain develops in a systematic, hierarchical manner, and requires certain "organizing experiences" at specific times in order to develop in a healthy way. Disruptions during critical periods, such as lack of sensory experience or abnormal neuronal activity due to extreme experiences, such as child maltreatment or trauma, may lead to major abnormalities or deficits in neurodevelopment (Cross, 2015; Perry, Pollard, Blakely, Baker, & Vigilante, 1995).

When a person perceives a threat, the mind and body have a deeply ingrained, primal response, very similar to those of other animals. An alarm is sounded, and the body prepares to fight or run away from the perceived threat, or freezes to become hidden. All noncritical information is tuned out, the person becomes hypervigilant, the heart rate increases, and the body diverts its energy to muscles and respiration in preparation for action. In the case of the child who has experienced trauma, this reaction may be activated by anything that reminds him or her of the traumatic event, or simply by thinking about it. The child may have this state consistently activated. Over time, the child may be in the fear response state so frequently, that he or she may remain in a persistent state of whole-body hyperarousal (Cross, 2015; Perry, 2009; Perry et al., 1995).

As the child grows, his or her brain catalogs what is safe in the surrounding environment. If there has not been safety with his or her first human contact with caretakers, especially, and then with others in the community, or if the brain assesses that the environment is not a safe one (as might happen when there have been episodes of community violence), his or her stress system will be activated in more situations. New environments and new people, especially people who are very different in appearance and behavior from family members, may create a powerful stress response (Perry, 2009). For many children, a common stress response is freezing, which appears to many adults, teachers for example, like oppositional-defiant behavior. In this situation, the child freezes (seems to refuse to comply) and does not respond to instructions he or she has been given. This usually results in the teacher giving the instruction again, but this time with a threat of what will happen if the child does not comply. The child will quickly move from feeling anxious to feeling threatened to feeling terrorized and might completely dissociate or disengage mentally from reality in order to protect himself from what is happening (Perry et al., 1995).

Dr. Gordon Hodas (2006), child psychiatric consultant to the state of Pennsylvania, outlines the following common beliefs from clinical observations of and conversations with children who have experienced trauma:

"The world is threatening and bewildering."
"The world is punitive, judgmental, humiliating and blaming."
"Control is external, not internal." Therefore, "I don't have control over my life."
"People are unpredictable. Very few are to be trusted."
"When challenged, I must defend myself—my honor, and my self-respect. Above all else, I must defend my honor—at any price."
"If I admit a mistake, things will be worse than if I don't."

Children who have experienced trauma often appear angry, aggressive, distrustful, isolated, oppositional, have difficulty understanding others' points of view, have difficulty regulating their emotions, have difficulty expressing their wishes and desires, are withdrawn, impulsive, inattentive, have difficulty completing tasks, lack sustained curiosity, have low self-esteem, and have feelings of guilt and shame (Cross, 2015). In a school setting, this behavior is confusing to school administrators, teachers, and staff, especially when there are multiple children exhibiting this behavior.

Without a trauma-informed lens for viewing this behavior, many school systems' responses to this behavior is punitive and has the expectation that children exhibiting this behavior will become intrinsically motivated to change their behavior, if disciplined severely enough. Additionally, in many schools where the teachers, staff, and administrators are from a different race, ethnicity, social economic status, and community than the children, there are even bigger barriers in these adults' understanding the types of trauma to which children may have been exposed, and these adults often come with their own biases about the children with whom they work, which impact their day to day interactions with their students.

According to the U.S. Department of Education Office for Civil Rights (2014a), in the 2011–2012 school year, African American students were suspended and expelled nationally from public schools at a rate 3 times greater than White students. On average, 5% of White students were suspended, compared to 16% of African American students. In just preschool alone, African American children represented 18% of total preschoolers, yet 48% of preschoolers receiving more than one out-of-school suspension, compared to White children who represented 43% of total preschool enrollment but only 26% of preschoolers receiving more than one out-of-school suspension. While African American students represent 16% of total enrollment, they represent 27% of students referred to law enforcement, and 31% of students experiencing a school-related arrest. These numbers increase for African American children identified as students with disabilities and being served under the Individuals with Disabilities Education Act (IDEA). For example, while African American students represent 19% of students with disabilities being served under IDEA, they are 36% of those restrained in school by a mechanical device or some type of equipment designed to restrict their freedom of movement.

Not every African American child in school is experiencing traumatic stress; even in communities where children are exposed to multiple risk factors. Yet, African American students are seen as more aggressive, disciplined more harshly for the same behaviors than are White students, and disciplined severely for minor infractions like disrespect, lack of compliance, and tardiness. Teacher and administrator racial bias accounts for much of this disproportionate application of discipline (Horner, Fireman, & Wang, 2010; Skiba, Chung, Trachok, Baker, & Sheya, 2014; Skiba et al., 2011). For children who have experienced trauma, exposure to a school system that appears hostile and unfair may be yet another source of traumatic stress.

SCHOOLS AS A RESPONSIVE PLACE
FOR TRAUMATIZED YOUTH

It is not surprising that African American children who have been exposed to trauma often struggle in school. They frequently have problems with trusting school staff and other students, completing school work, focusing during instruction, and following rules (Langley, Gonzalez, Sugar, Solis, & Jaycox, 2015). The difficulties African American children face in school can have long-term effects on their ability to achieve success. For some, school failure can result in dropping out of school or engaging in disruptive school behaviors (Hurt, Malmud, Brodsky, & Giannetta, 2001). What follows is a series of solutions school districts might consider in order to make the transition from being *trauma uninformed* to becoming *trauma informed* to becoming *trauma responsive*.

Schools have to become part of the solution for children who have been exposed to trauma. Though this may be a complex task for schools, if it is not done, schools will become a place that retraumatizes children and not a place where students learn and grow (Nadeem, Jaycox, Kataoka, Langley, & Stein, 2011). Schools can function as a holistic community where children can learn how to trust adults and peers, so they can function in and out of the school setting. It is imperative that trauma-specific approaches to educational practices be developed for all schools so that they can meet the needs of children who have been exposed to trauma. Addressing trauma in schools must be a whole-school approach and not a series of interventions for individual children. A whole-school strategy is necessary to ensure that trauma-responsive approaches are woven into the fabric of the school. They should be a part of daily activities so that children feel safe academically, emotionally, and physically through out the school setting (Nadeem et al., 2011). If they become part of the fabric of the school, they will impact children who may be experiencing trauma but may not rise to the awareness of school staff, perhaps because they are quiet and compliant instead of acting out. These children, particularly, will benefit from a whole-school approach to trauma.

Developing a trauma-responsive space for youth is complex, and schools neither can nor should do this work alone. Collaborating with schools should be community resources such as mental health centers, child welfare agencies, community centers, institutions of higher education, advocacy organizations, and other stakeholders who must partner together to develop strategies and supports (Walkley & Cox, 2013). The community school model is a perfect example of how schools can bring together community partners, such as religious institutions, social service agencies, food pantries, universities, and other grassroots organizations to meet the day-to-day needs of families, such as housing, employment, substance abuse services, mental health services, and medical care.

With support, school staff can become the lifeline to children who have experienced trauma, but this will require an entire system of support within schools and from outside of schools. This may be done by supporting the following six activities:

1. Training educators and school staff about trauma
2. Creating clinical support systems for schools
3. Reexamining school policies
4. Adapting school curricula to be trauma responsive
5. Developing procedures for early identification and services
6. Funding trauma responsive collaboration

Training educators and school staff about trauma

In order to stop the retraumatization of African American children in schools, teachers and other school staff must be provided with ongoing training and support to be able to understand and identify the symptoms of trauma and its impact on children of color (Dorsey, Briggs, & Woods, 2011; Oehlberg, 2008). This is a critical beginning step in developing a whole-school approach to developing a trauma-responsive educational environment. Trauma-responsive training in schools, at a minimum, should include defining trauma; impact of trauma on brain development and learning; short-term and long-term impacts of trauma; and school staff's impact on childhood trauma. However, training cannot be a "one and done" approach. It must be infused throughout all trainings and become an institutional part of practice. Trauma-responsive education should not be an add-on or tool in a teacher's arsenal but should be an inclusive approach to educating the whole child (Carello & Butler, 2015). Teachers also need to learn about their own trauma (both what they brought to the job and what they developed from working in a difficult environment), how their students may trigger it, and how it may trigger their students.

Washington State is one of the leaders in the trauma responsive school movement (Stevens, 2012). In Washington State they have developed a trauma responsive infrastructure called "Compassionate Schools: The Heart of Learning and Teaching." A key component of the Compassionate Schools infrastructure is training educators. Their training framework is based on the companion book *The Heart of Learning and Teaching: Compassion, Resiliency, and Academic Success*. The training is broken into four broad sections: background on trauma, compassion, and resiliency; teacher self-care; classroom strategies; and school community partnerships (Washington State Superintendent of Public Instruction Office, 2011).

Creating clinical support systems for schools

The creation of clinical supports for schools is important. Schools need to have access to clinical supports to assist in the development of effective classroom-wide strategies for addressing the needs of children who may have been exposed to trauma in a way that does not have an adverse impact (Langley et al., 2015). It often goes unrecognized by both school administrators and teachers themselves that they are working with several traumatized children each day. In an effort to provide quality instruction there is a need for clinical experts to provide input to school-based staff in the development of classroom strategies based on the individual needs of their students (Fazel, Hoagwood, Stephan, & Ford, 2014). Another benefit of providing direct clinical support to teachers is the assistance it may provide directly to teachers who themselves have experienced trauma. Often the teachers' personal experiences are not addressed, which can impact their ability to teach their students. The school environment can also be retraumatizing for school staff and if not recognized can have long-lasting impacts on them and their students (Bussey, 2008; Knight, 2010). If school staff has access to clinicians, they can request support in handling their own responses to encountering similar children in their classrooms (Fazel et al., 2014).

Reexamining school policies

School systems need to intentionally reevaluate school policies in light of the needs of traumatized children. It is important that policies on confidentiality, discipline, and instruction be reexamined to ensure they meet the needs of all children (Finkelhor, Ormrod, Turner, & Hamby, 2012). School systems need to ensure policies, such as reporting child abuse, interactions with parents, safety planning, and schoolwide interventions and practices, are trauma responsive (Finkelhor et al., 2012). School discipline policies are trauma responsive when they balance accountability with an understanding of traumatic behavior. For example, including discipline strategies that promote positive behavioral interventions and strategies, encourage prevention, and embrace restorative practices, shift discipline from a punitive process to one that is more supportive in nature (U.S. Department of Education, 2014b).

Adapting school curricula to be trauma responsive

Schools need to adapt instructional curricula and materials to be trauma responsive. Educational researchers have just begun to critically examine trauma-specific methods for teaching core subject areas such as reading, writing, and math (Carello & Butler, 2015; Courtois & Gold, 2009). However, research exists indicating that children who have experienced trauma can benefit from interactive teaching approaches (Courtois & Gold, 2009).

Recent studies on childhood trauma have established that a child's body keeps track of traumatic memories (Perry, 2009). The neurobiological effects of experiencing trauma are clearly as impactful as the emotional effects (Perry, 2009). This research will have implications for instructional curriculum as it pertains to the importance of physical education and arts programming in both elementary and secondary schools. School systems and educational curriculum developers need to enhance and create innovative curriculum in the core subject areas that incorporate these findings. This research may have vast implications for educational curricula, particularly as it attests to the value of physical education and arts programs in elementary and secondary schools. Innovative curriculum development in academic areas, such as reading, that incorporate these new findings must be piloted and funded at the state and local levels (Carello & Butler, 2015).

In addition to overall changes to reform curricula to be trauma responsive, educators should incorporate conflict-resolution skills and the development of empathy into the regular instruction (West, Day, Somers, & Baroni, 2014). If children who have been exposed to trauma continue to develop the ability to understand and deal with the perspectives of peers and adults, they may be more capable of responding to situations appropriately. Conflict-resolution skills help children understand and name their emotions (West et al., 2014).

Developing procedures for early identification and services

Since the development of trauma-responsive curricula is in the beginning phases, schools must develop procedures and protocols for early identification of children who have experienced trauma. School systems may offer opportunities for school psychologists, social workers, school-based mental health clinicians, and families to partner with educators to identify these practices (Walkley & Cox, 2013). Together they can also develop effective school-based mental health interventions for serving this population. In order to see lasting impact, it is imperative that interventions focus on the entire family (Langley et al., 2015). Serving the child alone will not be effective. Every attempt should be made to serve the entire family, at home, if possible, in order to address the entire system (Oehlberg, 2008). This can be done systemwide but should also be done on the individual school level. Each school community has its own culture, and schools must ensure that interventions respect the culture and the confidentiality and safety needs of these children and their families.

In addition to developing protocols for early identification, school systems need to take a look at special education evaluations. These evaluations must also be trauma responsive and consider the traumatic aspects of a child's disabilities and offer trauma-related services as necessary. Special education teams must work collaboratively to appropriately diagnose the symptoms of trauma (Perry, 2009). Schools need to be careful not to misdiagnose traumatic symptoms as attention deficit hyperactivity disorder (ADHD), emotional disturbances, or other learning disabilities, or vice versa (Perry, 2009). Misdiagnosis can result in the retraumatization of children or the development of programs that fail to meet their needs because they do not address the traumatic symptoms interfering with the child's ability to access instruction (Langley et al., 2015).

Funding trauma-responsive collaboration

School systems must have adequate funding at the local level to support the trauma responsive work that must be done. Funding must be provided for the development of community-based services that will meet the needs schools are facing. These funds should be allocated to organizations that can bring together experts to collaboratively problem-solve and develop community-based, trauma-responsive strategies. In order for schools to become trauma responsive, it is important to have opportunities for teachers, school-based mental health clinicians, parents, and school administrators to be able to collaborate directly, without fiscal or confidentiality barriers (Carello & Butler, 2015).

IMPLEMENTING TRAUMA RESPONSIVE APPROACHES IN SCHOOLS

Becoming a trauma responsive school takes organizational change. It is not something that happens overnight but takes time and a philosophical paradigm shift to occur and be sustained overtime (Carello & Butler, 2015). When a school becomes trauma responsive it provides an educational environment that is safe, stable, and understanding for students, staff, and families (Nadeem et al., 2011). The main goal is to prevent retraumatization. Two states, Massachusetts and Washington, have undertaken a full-scale system approach to creating trauma-responsive schools. A description of these states' approaches by Stevens (2012) follows.

Massachusetts

The work in Massachusetts began with a statewide policy agenda in 2005. Through the policy work, the state launched "Helping Traumatized Children Learn." Instead of adopting a rigid model, they adopted a flexible framework that allowed schools to implement a variety of trauma-sensitive practices and supports. The framework was comprised of six domains: school culture and infrastructure; staff training; links to mental health professionals; academic instruction for students who have experienced trauma; nonacademic strategies; and school policies, procedure, and protocols.

In addition to the implementation of the flexible framework, Massachusetts used a legislative platform to encourage funding support for this work. They were able to successfully legislate the development of a grant fund to support the implementation of trauma-responsive interventions and supports in schools. Through these funds, schools were able to develop and implement innovative strategies to train staff and support students and families within their schools.

Massachusetts continues to implement a systemwide trauma-responsive schools system. It has been able to sustain this practice through the support of the Trauma Committee that was created to provide guidance and technical assistance to schools. The system continues to assess the needs of the children and families it serves in an effort to ensure the strategies align.

Washington State

Washington has worked collaboratively to bring attention to the needs of children who have experienced trauma. They have developed resources and tools that are currently being used in many states. Washington calls its trauma responsive approach the "Compassionate Schools Initiative." It has released the handbook *The Heart of Learning and Teaching: Compassion, Resiliency, and Academic Success.* The book provides an overview of trauma in schools, importance of self-care, and outlines six principles that should guide interactions with children who have experienced trauma. The six guiding principles are always empower, never disempower; provide unconditional positive regard; maintain high expectations; check assumptions, observe, and question; be a relationship coach; and provide guided opportunities for helpful participation. The Compassionate Schools Initiative has developed a series of training modules that can be accessed by the public and used along with the handbook.

INVOLVING FAMILY AND COMMUNITY

Research has shown that closeness to and involvement with family members provides protective factors for African American children and youth exposed to risk factors, such as community violence and other types of trauma (Hammack, Richards, Luo, Edlynn, & Roy, 2004; Henry, Lambert, & Smith Bynum, 2015). The community, and the social supports within it, also provide strong supports for children and families, and may help to counteract some of the effects of the risk to which children are exposed (Eachus, 2014; Nebbitt, Lombe, Yu, Vaughn, & Stokes, 2012). For this reason, engaging parents and community members as important assets and stakeholders should be an integral component of transitioning a school or school system from being *trauma uninformed* to becoming *trauma informed* to being *trauma responsive*. Developing trusted partnerships with parents and community members, which will allow for open discussions about the risk factors to which children are exposed, will be educational for school administrators and staff, provide them with valuable insight into what children and families need, and will help them avoid potential pitfalls created by their ignorance of community norms and realities.

This type of organizational transformation will require a complete change in thinking for many school leaders. It requires expanding educators' ideas of what happens in school; that school is about more than reading, writing, and math. It requires widening many educators' thoughts about who is required to sit on the team to help a child learn; that team now includes a range of partners, including clinicians, parents, and community members. It requires setting a standard within schools for teachers and school staff that punitive discipline is not acceptable, because it does not achieve positive results, but alienates some children and pushes them into a school-to-prison pipeline from which there is no return. It requires shifting from a paradigm where adults ask children, "What's wrong with you?" to one where adults ask children, "What has happened to you?" (National Center for Trauma Informed Care, 2015).

REFERENCES

Ackerman, B. P., & Izard, C. E. (1999). Contextual risk, caregiver emotionality, and the problem behaviors of six- and seven-year-old from economically disadvantaged families. *Child Development, 70*(6), 1415–1427.

Appleyard, K., Egeland, B., VanDulmen, M. H., & Sroufe, L. A. (2005). When more is not better: The role of cumulative risk in child behavior outcomes. *Journal of Child Psychology & Psychiatry, 46*(3), 235–245. doi:10.1111/j.1469-7610.2004.00351.x

Bussey, M. C. (2008). Trauma response and recovery certificate program: Preparing students for effective practice. *Journal of Teaching in Social Work, 28*(1–2), 117–144. doi:10.1080/08841230802179118

Carello, J., & Butler, L. D. (2015). Practicing what we teach: Trauma-informed educational practice. *Journal of Teaching in Social Work, 35*(3), 262–278. doi:10.1080/08841233.2015.1030059

Centers for Disease Control. (2010). Adverse childhood experiences reported by adults: Five states, 2009. *Morbidity and Mortality Weekly Report (MMWR), 59*(49).

Courtois, C. A., & Gold, S. N. (2009). The need for inclusion of psychological trauma in the professional curriculum: A call to action. *Psychological Trauma: Theory, Research, Practice, and Policy, 1*(1), 3–23. doi:10.1037/a0015224

Cross, K. (2015). *Complex trauma in early childhood.* Retrieved from http://www.aaets.org/article174.htm

Crusto, C. A., Whitson, M. L., Walling, S. M., Feinn, R., Friedman, S. R., Reynolds, J., Kaufman, J. S. (2010). Posttraumatic stress among young urban children exposed to family violence and other potentially traumatic events. *Journal of Traumatic Stress, 23*(6), 716–724. doi:10.1002/jts.20590

Dorsey, S., Briggs, E. C., & Woods, B. A. (2011). Cognitive-behavioral treatment for posttraumatic stress disorder in children and adolescents. *Child and Adolescent Psychiatric Clinics of North America, 20*, 255–269. doi:10.1016/j.chc.2011.01.006

Drake, B., & Rank, M. R. (2009). The racial divide among American children in poverty: Reassessing the importance of neighborhood. *Children and Youth Services Review, 31*(12), 1264–1271.

Eachus, P. (2014). Community resilience: Is it greater than the sum of the parts of individual resilience? *Procedia Economics and Finance, 18*, 345–351.

Fazel, M., Hoagwood, K., Stephan, S., & Ford, T. (2014). Series: Mental health interventions in schools in high-income countries. *The Lancet Psychiatry, 1*, 377–387. doi:10.1016/S2215-0366(14)70312-8

Felitti, V. J., Anda, R. F., Nordenberg, D., Williamson, D. F., Spitz, A. M., Edwards, V., & Marks, J. S. (1998). Relationship of childhood abuse and household dysfunction to many of the leading causes of death in adults: The adverse childhood experiences (ACE) study. *American Journal of Preventive Medicine, 14*(4), 245–258.

Finkelhor, D., Ormrod, R., Turner, H., & Hamby, S. (2012). Child and youth victimization known to police, school, and medical authorities. National Survey of Children's Exposure to Violence. *Juvenile Justice Bulletin.* Retrieved from http://www.ojjdp.gov/pubs/235394.pdf

Finkelhor, D., Shattuck, A., Turner, H., & Hamby, S. (2015). A revised inventory of Adverse Childhood Experiences. *Child Abuse & Neglect, 48*(October), 13–21.

Finkelhor, J., Turner, H., Ormrod, R., & Hamby, S. (2009). Violence, abuse and crime exposure in a national sample of children and youth. *Pediatrics, 124*(5), 1411–1423.

Hammack, P. L., Richards, M. H., Luo, Z., Edlynn, E. S., & Roy, K. (2004). Social support factors as moderators of community violence exposure among inner-city African American young adolescents. *Journal of Clinical Child and Adolescent Psychology: The Official Journal for the Society of Clinical Child And Adolescent Psychology, American Psychological Association, Division 53, 33*(3), 450–462.

Henry, J. S., Lambert, S. F., & Smith Bynum, M. (2015). The protective role of maternal racial socialization for African American adolescents exposed to community violence. *Journal of Family Psychology, 29*(4), 548–557. doi:10.1037/fam0000135

Hodas, G. R. (2006). *Responding to childhood trauma: The promise and practice of trauma informed care.* Retrieved from http://www.nsvrc.org/publications/reports/responding-childhood-trauma-promise-and-practice-trauma-informed-care

Horner, S. B., Fireman, G. D., & Wang, E. W. (2010). The relation of student behavior, peer status, race, and gender to decisions about school discipline using CHAID decision trees and regression modeling. *Journal of School Psychology*, *48*(2), 135–161.

Hurt, H., Malmud, E., Brodsky, N. L., & Giannetta, J. (2001). Exposure to violence: Psychological and academic correlates in child witnesses. *Archives of Pediatrics & Adolescent Medicine*, *155*(12), 1351–1356.

Knight, C. (2010). Indirect trauma in the field practicum: Secondary traumatic stress, vicarious trauma, and compassion fatigue among social work students and their field instructors. *Journal of Baccalaureate Social Work*, *15*(1), 31–52.

Langley, A. K., Gonzalez, A., Sugar, C. A., Solis, D., & Jaycox, L. (2015). Bounce back: Effectiveness of an elementary school-based intervention for multicultural children exposed to traumatic events. *Journal of Consulting and Clinical Psychology*, *83*(5), 853–865. doi:10.1037/ccp0000051

McLoyd, V. C. (1990). The impact of economic hardship on Black families and children: Psychological distress, parenting, and socioemotional development. *Child Development*, *61*(2), 311–346.

Nadeem, E., Jaycox, L. H., Kataoka, S. H., Langley, A. K., & Stein, B. D. (2011). Going to scale: Experiences implementing a school-based trauma intervention. *School Psychology Review*, *40*(4), 549–568.

National Center for Trauma Informed Care. (2015). *Purpose and mission of NCTIC*. Retrieved from http://www.samhsa.gov/nctic/about

National Child Traumatic Stress Network. (2015). *Defining trauma and child traumatic stress*. Retrieved from http://www.nctsn.org/content/defining-trauma-and -child-traumatic-stress

Nebbitt, V. E., Lombe, M., Yu, M., Vaughn, M. G., & Stokes, C. (2012). Ecological correlates of substance use in African American adolescents living in public housing communities: Assessing the moderating effects of social cohesion. *Children and Youth Services Review*, *34*(2), 338–347.

Oehlberg, B. (2008). Why schools need to be trauma informed. *Trauma and Loss: Research and Interventions*, *8*(2), 12–15.

Perry, B. D. (2009). Examining child maltreatment through a neurodevelopmental lens: Clinical applications of the neurosequential model of therapeutics. *Journal of Loss & Trauma*, *14*(4), 240–255. doi:10.1080/15325020903004350

Perry, B. D., Pollard, R. A., Blakley, T. L., Baker, W. L., & Vigilante, D. (1995). Childhood trauma, the neurobiology of adaptation, and "use-dependent" development of the brain: How "states" become "traits." *Infant Mental Health Journal*, *16*(4), 271–291.

Ricketts, E. R., & Sawhill, I. V. (1988). Defining and measuring the underclass. *Journal of Policy Analysis and Management*, *7*(2), 316–325.

Sessoms, N. J., & Wolch, J. R. (2008). Measuring concentrated poverty in a global metropolis: Lessons from Los Angeles. *Professional Geographer*, *60*(1), 70–86.

Skiba, R. J., Chung, C., Trachok, M., Baker, T., & Sheya, A. (2014). Parsing disciplinary disproportionality: Contributions of infraction, student, and school characteristics to out-of-school suspension and expulsion. *American Educational Research Journal*, *51*(4), 640–670.

Skiba, R. J., Horner, R. H., Chung, C.-G., Rausch, M. K., May, S. L., & Tobin, T. (2011). Race is not neutral: A national investigation of African American and Latino disproportionality in school discipline. *School Psychology Review*, *40*(1), 85–107.

Slep, A. M. S., & O'Leary, S. G. (2005). Parent and partner violence in families with young children: Rates, patterns, and connections. *Journal of Consulting and Clinical Psychology*, *73*(3), 435–444. doi:10.1037/0022-006X.73.3.435

Stevens, J. E. (2012). *Massachusetts, Washington State lead U.S. trauma-sensitive school movement.* Retrieved from http://acestoohigh.com/2012/05/31/massachusetts -washington-state-lead-u-s-trauma-sensitive-school-movement/

U.S. Department of Education. (2014a). Data snapshot: School discipline. *Issue Brief No. 1, March.* Retrieved from http://ocrdata.ed.gov/Downloads/CRDC-School -Discipline-Snapshot.pdf

U.S. Department of Education. (2014b). *Guiding principles: A resource guide for improving school climate and discipline.* Washington, DC: U.S. Department of Education.

Wadsworth, M. E., & Berger, L. E. (2006). Adolescents coping with poverty-related family stress: Prospective predictors of coping and psychological symptoms. *Journal of Youth & Adolescence, 35*(1), 54-67. doi:10.1007/s10964-005-9022-5

Wadsworth, M. E., & Santiago, C. D. (2008). Risk and resiliency processes in ethnically diverse families in poverty. *Journal of Family Psychology, 22*(3), 399–410. doi:10.1037/0893-3200.22.3.399

Walkley, M., & Cox, T. L. (2013). Building trauma-informed schools and communities. *Children & Schools, 35*(2), 123–126.

Washington State Superintendent of Public Instruction Office. (2011). *Compassionate schools: The heart of learning and teaching.* Retrieved from http://www.k12.wa.us /CompassionateSchools/default.aspx

West, S. D., Day, A. G., Somers, C. L., & Baroni, B. A. (2014). Student perspectives on how trauma experiences manifest in the classroom: Engaging court-involved youth in the development of a trauma-informed teaching curriculum. *Children and Youth Services Review, 38*, 58–65. doi:10.1016/j.childyouth.2014.01.013

Yang, R., & Jargowsky, P. A. (2006). Suburban development and economic segregation in the 1990s. *Journal of Urban Affairs, 28*(3), 253–273.

7 Peace, be still

Black educators coping with constant school reforms in Philadelphia

Camika Royal

> I started teaching as a very energetic person who wanted to work with kids and just knew that education was what I wanted to do. But the closer you get to the top and the more you realize the politics, about the politics of education, sometimes it's challenging to remain positive and not become cynical. And the politics of education is [*sic*] so strong that it's almost devastating.
>
> Retired Black Philadelphia educator[1]

Black[2] public school educators in Philadelphia have been essential, vulnerable, and dubious almost since the School District of Philadelphia (SDP) began in 1818. By 2009, SDP's Black student population remained steady for years at about 70%, while Black educators had declined from 36% in 1978 to 29% (Dean, 2008). This chapter explores Black Philadelphia educators' resilience and efficacy as they navigated education policy reforms and school district politics from 1967 to 2007, through six superintendents, chronic underfunding and instability, a series of strikes, and a state takeover. In the Holy Bible, Jesus Christ and his disciples were caught in a dangerous storm on a boat, and they asked him, "Teacher, do You not care that we are perishing?" He responded to them, "Peace, be still," and when the storm calmed, he chastised their fear and lack of faith in the storm (Mark 4:38–40 New King James Version). Essentially, these Black educators demonstrated the type of peace and faith in the midst of their professional uncertainty and chaos that Jesus Christ urged of his disciples.

Studies conducted of urban school reform have focused on the impact on students or students' academic performances, not the educators who intermediate reforms and intended outcomes (e.g., Cuban & Usdan, 2003; Tyack & Cuban, 1995). Michele Foster (1991, p. 239), who pioneered research on Black teachers, lamented that "the paucity of contemporary accounts by African Americans about their ... experiences ... will limit current and future historians'

---

1 Interview, July 29, 2010.
2 *Black* and *African American* are used interchangeably in this chapter.

and sociologists' complete understanding of schools and schooling." Dingus (2006) elucidated the presence and impact of community reciprocity on three generations of Black educators throughout their professional socialization. Building on the work of Foster and Dingus, this chapter examines how Black educators understood their jobs, the school district, and themselves in the district. This chapter also explores how the professional situations of Black educators were influenced by the policies, practices, and politics of the school and school district in which these educators worked.

Philadelphia matters in the national landscape of urban school reform. It has the second oldest public school system in the nation, and in its schooling for Black students and treatment of Black educators, public schools in Philadelphia have been rife with racialized policies and practices almost since its inception almost 200 years ago (Foster, 1990). Black public school educators in Philadelphia have always been subject to the political will of those with the authority to create, color, or dismantle their work with the stroke of a pen. In *The Education of Black Philadelphia*, V. P. Franklin (1979, p. xvii) wrote, "changes in the public education of black Philadelphia in the twentieth century were inextricably tied to larger social, political, and economic changes for blacks in the city—improvements in race relations, increases in black political power, economic depressions, and the like."

More than one hundred years after the school district began, SDP ended its de jure, racist hiring practices when it merged its race-based lists of eligible teachers, though it maintained de facto practices of preferential positions for White educators (Franklin, 1979; Hayre & Moore, 1997). Since the 1960s, these professional issues between SDP and Black educators have remained, even as pressure and stresses have increased for urban public school districts, including Philadelphia (see Birger, 1996; Cuban & Usdan, 2003; Dixson, Royal, & Henry, 2014; Phillips, 2005; Wong & Shen, 2003). Urban schools are especially vulnerable given their conditions and their extreme needs (Anyon, 2005; B. A. Jones, 2005; Kozol, 1991; Noguera, 2003). Schools and school district–based hierarchies often have adversarial work environments and cultures with which many educators cope by closing their doors to the chaos (Ingersoll, 2003; Wilms, 2003). This is exacerbated in urban schools and districts.

Due to instructional surveillance and demands to yield high test scores from students regardless of contexts, the most exceptional teachers may opt out of teaching in the neediest urban schools, while the professional climate in these schools tend toward negative (Murrell, 2000; Nieto, 2003; Weiner, 1999). Schools with lower achievement and high poverty rates have higher teacher attrition rates (Bobek, 2002; Ingersoll, 2001; Mac Iver & Vaughn, 2007; Neild, Useem, & Farley, 2005; Neild, Useem, Travers, & Lesnick, 2003; Useem, Offenberg, & Farley, 2007). Teachers have become even more scrutinized as school systems attempt to foolproof schooling systems through stringent, standardized, mechanized, and heavily scripted curricula (Nieto, 2003). These efforts neither inspire nor encourage teachers to perform better at their jobs (Wilms, 2003). Rather, they demoralize teachers, devalue their work, and make educators weary (Dworkin, 2001; Moore, 2012). Weariness can wreak havoc on school culture, causing or reinforcing various emotional responses in educators, impacting how they view the profession, themselves in the profession, and how they view students (Aronson, 2004; Rex & Nelson, 2004; Taylor, 2006). For example, in September 2013, after mass layoffs of Philadelphia's public school assistant principals, counselors, nurses, librarians, and secretaries, a very frustrated veteran teacher penned an open letter to the mayor and governor in *The Philadelphia Daily News* regarding her professional situation. She wrote:

> Come into my third grade class and show me how to teach 32 children ... to do reading groups ... that will improve instruction ... how to teach a math program without workbooks and paper ... how to organize my day so I am not just disciplining the children ... I am only one person.[3]

There is a relationship between educators' attitudes, beliefs about their work, and the context in which they work, especially when the negative climate in urban schools/districts often leave teachers questioning their efficacy (Hargreaves, 1996; Weiner, 1999). The following elements all relate to educators' beliefs about their work: educational backgrounds and familial rearing; personal educational philosophies; race; gender; the social, historical, and political context of work; school and school district culture; and national and state education policies (Agee, 2004; Foster, 1991; Lynn, 2006; Rex & Nelson, 2004). Historically, Black educators have found White colleagues to have lower expectations for Black students, and numerous studies have pointed to conflicts between Black and White educators regarding Black students and other areas of their work (e.g., Delpit, 1995; Foster, 1997; Franklin, 1979; Gordon, 2000; Hayre & Moore, 1997; Oates, 2003). Other studies have demonstrated Black educators' competence being questioned by their colleagues and students (Allen, Jacobson, & Lomotey, 1995; Foster, 1990; Milner & Hoy, 2003). Conversely, both C. Jones (2002) and Dingus (2006) found positive personal and professional relationships between and among Black educators and with Black communities. Considering how educators may experience the profession and school district differently according to their racial affiliation, Agee (2004, p. 770) acknowledges that there is a gap between educators' constructed identities and "politics of teaching in public schools." Black urban educators identify deeply with the communities in which they work, serve as cultural translators and intercessors for Black

---

3 Though the letter is no longer available online, the author saved the contents of the letter when it was initially published. Additionally, Willner can be heard discussing her open letter here, retrieved January 7, 2016: http://www.newsworks.org/index.php/local/education/60156 -ogontz-teacher-discusses-frustrated-letters-she-sent-to-pa-gov-and-phila-mayor

students, act as social agents who see the inequity of school systems but are not overwhelmed by it, are culturally and politically relevant instructors, and are tokens who make the most of their tokenized professional situations (Beauboeuf-Lafontant, 2002; Irvine, 1989; Kelly, 2007; Ladson-Billings, 1994; Stanford, 1997).

This work began with the assumption that race narratives matter in education, particularly the experiential knowledge of Black educators as central to understanding the sociopolitical context of urban school systems (Matsuda, Lawrence, Delgado, & Crenshaw, 1993). Critical race theory, narrative identity theory, and resilience theory are the lenses through which this work was approached. Social reality is constructed through ongoing interactions, specifically through narratives (Berger & Luckmann, 1967; Ladson-Billings & Tate, 1995). People make sense of their lives through the stories they tell about them (Bruner, 1991, 1998). Identities are socially and historically constructed, context matters, and one needs a narrative in order to process one's identity (Vila, 2000).

The professional context combined with stress-yielding elements of urban schools may be related to educators' resilience and the decisions they make to stay or leave the education profession (Anyon, 2005; Bobek, 2002; Moore, 2012; Patterson, Collins, & Abbott, 2004). Resilience is a process developed throughout interactions between the person and their environment (Bobek, 2002). Educators are resilient when they use "energy productively to achieve school goals in the face of adverse conditions"; "in urban schools, teacher and teacher leader resilience is critical to schools accomplishing what needs to be done" (Patterson et al., 2004, p. 3). Nieto (2003) argued that what makes great educators stay is the impact they know they have on their students and school communities. Still, issues of race in schools and school districts can influence how educators interpret their work culture and their definitions of their professional situations (Milner & Hoy, 2003).

This chapter comes from a larger study (Royal, 2012) that used historical documents from Temple University's Urban Archives, oral histories from Philadelphia community members, and Black educator interviews. Of the 20 self-identified Black educators interviewed as key narrators, there were 15 women and 5 men who worked in the district between 10 to 37 years. On average, they worked in SDP for 26 years. Sixteen of these Black educators were educated in SDP.

When superintendent Mark Shedd arrived in Philadelphia in 1967, African Americans had felt underserved and disrespected by the White school district power structure for years. White ethnics believed that any educational advance for Blacks represented a loss for them and their children. While Blacks were initially skeptical of this newcomer and Philadelphia outsider, Black educators remembered him as having brought new energy and fresh excitement about possibilities in urban education, generally, and for Philadelphia, specifically. Shedd was a well-trained innovator who made opportunities available to people who had previously been denied them, specifically African Americans.

He attempted to distinguish himself from Philadelphia's history of racialized practices, but he was not immune to the city's racial politics. Racial tensions throughout the city, the protest at SDP's administration building early in Shedd's administration, and ongoing disagreements with the teachers' union and police commissioner-turned-mayor Frank Rizzo led to Shedd's resignation in 1971 (Birger, 1996; Countryman, 2006).

Mayor Rizzo chose two Philadelphia insiders to succeed Shedd in leading SDP: Matthew Costanzo and Michael Marcase. Costanzo's tenure was riddled with teacher layoffs, a series of strikes, and lawsuits for failure to desegregate schools. When he left his post in 1975, SDP had a $27 million budget deficit and was facing battles with federal and state governments regarding the use of Title I funds and desegregation issues. Marcase, his successor, was constantly embroiled in controversies over his credentials and other improprieties. Racial politics were at their worst during the Marcase era; he was a nonrespected figurehead. There were constant financial problems, including a more than $230 million deficit, teacher furloughs, and the rescinding of their salary raises. During the Rizzo, Costanzo, and Marcase years, there was a lazy work culture and a lack of concern for and investment in teachers. Central administration of SDP was considered an old boys' network with a hierarchal structure through which people were promoted in lockstep so as not to disrupt the culture or structure of the empire. There were also several strikes during their tenures, one in 1972, which lasted 4 weeks, and one in 1981 that delayed the start of school until November. Black educators were heavily impacted by these strikes, both financially and collegially.

Marcase left the superintendence at the end of the school year in 1982, though he remained on the payroll for 2 additional years. After the financial chaos and professional decay that had eroded SDP, stakeholders were looking for a superintendent who would have everyone's respect and could bring pride and life back to the school district. That person was Constance Clayton. She was the first African American and the first woman superintendent, and many African Americans believed they could trust her with the education of their children (Royal, 2009). Black SDP educators held a nostalgic reverence for the Clayton era. According to them, SDP grew, flourished, and was made stronger during this time, largely attributed to her understanding Philadelphia personally, professionally, and racially, whereas other superintendents did not. As such, Clayton was believed to have provided stability for a system that had been in flux for years.

Depending on how success is measured, Constance Clayton was, arguably, the most successful superintendent of this modern era within SDP: new graduation requirements replaced the 1947 version; the first balanced budget since 1968 was achieved in her first year of leadership and maintained throughout her 11-year term; an improved bond rating; and no strikes. Still, Clayton's leadership style gave some people pause. Whereas they felt Shedd acted too quickly, some educators recalled Clayton's administration as bureaucratic and hierarchical; that it exhibited a lack of transparency; that there were policy implementation issues; and that she put undue pressure on principals and had no interoffice collaboration. Politically, Clayton also made people somewhat uncomfortable. In a system where political favors had been historically bought and sold, and superintendents were beholden to various political factions and entities, Clayton demanded otherwise. Though Clayton advocated the importance of merit in professional appointments, she also demonstrated an allegiance to, affinity for, and responsibility to African American professionals. Ironically, then, intraracial politics contributed to Clayton's exit. Rotan Lee, an ambitious African American on Philadelphia's Board of Education, forged alliances with Whites who opposed Clayton. While she had never let on that she was considering retirement, Lee had alluded to the potential for it on more than one occasion. She resigned unexpectedly in the summer of 1993.

David Hornbeck followed her as superintendent and began in 1994. Though he had built his career advocating for children, not all stakeholders in Philadelphia welcomed Hornbeck. Black educators hesitated to invest in his leadership, and this lack of investment caused him problems, initially. Many Black educators and community members saw Hornbeck as a poor politician, severely hindered by his lack of Philadelphia context. Though communication and political skill were not his strong points, many Black educators and other community members believed Hornbeck cared for children of color in Philadelphia. Hornbeck believed that SDP needed to change the way it did business. To that end, he restructured governance and management to focus on local control and more decentralization. Locally, though, school-based educators felt overwhelmed, overly burdened, and undersupported by Hornbeck's reforms.

There was an already longstanding contentious relationship between SDP and the Pennsylvania state legislature. During the Marcase administration, the adversarial nature of the relationship among the city, the district, and the state had become apparent when the state legislature changed its requirements for Philadelphia's superintendent in order to put Marcase in the position. Hornbeck's interpersonal communication and lack of political skill worsened the situation. During the Hornbeck administration, much of this contention centered on Hornbeck's lack of sufficient funds to fully implement his school reform model. Hornbeck, Mayor Ed Rendell, the school board, and city council tangled with Governor Tom Ridge and the state legislature for years regarding funding for SDP. By May 2000, the state had hired a search firm to look for a replacement for Hornbeck in the event a state takeover happened. By August 2000, Hornbeck had resigned.

The Commonwealth of Pennsylvania seized control of Philadelphia's public schools in December 2001. This state takeover made Philadelphia the first school district of its size to come under state control while simultaneously privatizing the management of many of its chronically underperforming schools (Useem, Christman, & Boyd, 2006). School takeover in Philadelphia was a political action, financial management and power, a demonstration of who was in charge. After battles between Mayor Street and Governor Schweiker, the new School Reform Commission would replace the long-standing Philadelphia Board of Education as the schools' governing body and would include five members, two appointed by the mayor and three appointed by the governor.

Former head of Chicago's public schools, Paul Vallas was appointed chief executive officer of SDP in 2002. There, he had been hailed as a "miracle worker." Though some credit Vallas with helping to heal political rifts between the city school system and the state left from years of dissonance, which were worsened during the Hornbeck era, many Black educators and other community members bemoaned Vallas' ability to lead Philadelphia's public schools given the questionable success of Chicago's public schools. More than anything, Black educators questioned Vallas' character traits and flaws, the magnanimous impressions he made while he was here. They described him as a snake oil salesman and a hustler; a conflicted politician who wanted to do well and to do good; a master communicator concerned with managing the impressions others had of him and his administration; a community-minded businessman who knew nothing about teaching and learning, and who made huge promises but left the district in severe debt. Most described him as a hype man whose substance had dissipated. Vallas was skillful in making powerful friends in high places. He made sure he got along with key people in the state legislature. He also built relationships with people on City Council. While some Black educators viewed Vallas as fearless and brave, unafraid of challenging characters and personalities in poor Black communities in Philadelphia, other Black educators viewed him as a bully.

Black educators also blamed Vallas for selling SDP's historic headquarters building. Since 1930, this edifice had served as the symbol of educational leadership in SDP, an impenetrable fortress into which Black professionals were not allowed. This began to change during Shedd's administration, and with Clayton's tenure, Black educators finally had access to the highest offices of this edifice from which they had been previously blocked. Black educators described the sale of this building as a collectively personal and professional loss. Furthermore, there was concern over the Vallas administration's use of quid pro quo contracts and misuse of funds. Vallas' financial management became a concern in October 2006 when the district's budget was found to be in deficit first by $21 million, then $70 million, then $73 million. Vallas never fully recovered his glowing public opinion after the budget deficit issue, and by the end of the 2006–2007 school year, Vallas was gone from the helm of SDP.

Impressions of SDP throughout the modern era of school reform, 1967–2007, vary significantly among Black educators. To some, it was considered too massive to manage effectively. Some describe it as not focused on children; instead, more focused on managing its public persona than improving educational outcomes for its children. Here are some Black educators' impressions of SDP:

> I'm asking myself *What is the District?* And so, you have the District: the downtown administration and their approach to schooling. And then you have the District: the schools and the teachers and the work that gets done in those classrooms. And unlike many charter school educators, I don't look at the District as a place where children are not cared about. I was a District educator. And I cared. And I know that there are good teachers in the District teaching their hearts out. I know there are good principals that are trying to do what they do in spite of the craziness from downtown … I think that there's tremendous talent in the District. But I don't think there's been tremendous leadership in a while.[4]

> There are only a few schools in this city that's [*sic*] really producing educated, well-educated students. The rest of them are just like a factory [*sic*] that's putting out inferior products. Then the kids are really are not ready to go out to a global society and function well.[5]

> From my position, and understand I'm speaking as a teacher, I question how much it is about our students. I look at the budget and how monies are spent. I look at administrators being placed in positions not to do the most good, but I don't know, just a warm body maybe. I personally think it's all about looking good on paper, even fudging it when you have to. Fudging documents you fill out. For instance, 89 percent of our kids came to school yesterday. No, they didn't. But if you do a certain kind of math you can make it look like 89 percent of the kids came to school and that's what the school district wants to see. That's not just at the school level, that's all the way up. Making it look good on paper but doing very little to make it a reality.[6]

> My opinion about the District depended on where I was working. And I think that's very significant. When you've got a huge district like Philadelphia, I personally and professionally don't think that those huge districts are *ever* going to be successful because you can't manage something that big. So what happens in Philadelphia: your experience becomes your Philadelphia. So, I was in good places. I was in places where people worked hard, knew what they were doing, were advocates for children, you know. And you start to think that's how it all is. So, from the time I started to the time I went to Central Office, my Philadelphia experience

4   Interview, July 12, 2010.
5   Interview, January 5, 2011.
6   Interview, June 17, 2010.

was very positive. Certainly I knew that there were problems, but you know, in a lot of the environments, I created the positivity, especially as a principal. You know, you're the leader of the building. But when I went downtown and then I saw what other people did and what other schools did and what was happening to children beyond my little sphere, that's when you really see the problems in Philadelphia.[7]

Black educators also positioned SDP as an unforgiving environment in which one error in judgment would follow someone throughout his or her career.

I think that one of the sad things that I have witnessed in the District is that incredibly smart, competent people can get in a little bit of trouble about whatever and they're just so marginalized that they can't be effective. And sometimes they leave, sometimes they just stay marginalized. And it seems like such a waste of talent to me.[8]

This is the bottom line: you can't do wrong [in the School District of Philadelphia].[9]

If you step out on your own ... and not pay due homage to the people over top of you, if you get sort of too big for your britches, you get knocked down all the way to, you know how on [*Who Wants to Be a*] *Millionaire*, whenever you're going for 50 but you get knocked all the way down to 5, there's a pattern of *get too big, and you're gonna get knocked down and out*. My guess would be that you'd have to commit a more serious thing to get knocked down if you're White. A lesser thing can get you knocked down if you're Black.[10]

But in Philadelphia, they have a tendency to hold onto stuff.[11]

These stories and descriptions of Philadelphia and its public school system bespeak the ways in which Black educators have made sense of SDP and thus defined their professional situations by these stories. The long racialized and political history of how SDP has dealt with Black educators, as well as its contradictions in policy and practice, have led to these professional narratives. The aforementioned long memory of people in Philadelphia and SDP compounds the political nature of the district, the politics, and power plays that govern its policies, practices, and professional culture. It impedes professional

7 Interview, July 27, 2010.
8 Interview, August 19, 2010.
9 Interview, July 22, 2010.
10 Interview, June 21, 2010.
11 Interview, July 29, 2010.

educators' desire to take risks on behalf of their students, school, and community (Royal & Gibson, in press). It encourages them to be safe, to minimize professional or ethical risk within SDP or to bear the possibility of being forever professionally marred in Philadelphia.

The professional culture of a school and school system is based on the people, the practices, and the politics that govern them. This, and Black educators' resilience, can best be seen in how they dealt with strikes in the 1970s and 1980s, when tensions were often drawn along racial lines. Some Black educators taught anyhow. They believed Black children should not be political pawns and deserved to be in school (Royal, 2009). Some taught in community-based alternate education sites. Those who crossed the picket lines to teach in public schools and those who taught in community-based alternate education sites saw themselves as advocating for students, especially high school seniors who needed academic credits to graduate. Some did not cross the picket lines to go into schools to work, but they empathized with those who did. Some did not want to antagonize colleagues by going into SDP schools, so they stayed away from picketing altogether. For many Black educators, choosing to strike or not to strike was a financial decision.

> It was very painful for me because I was a young person who didn't have a lot of money. So first of all, teachers are broke people. I didn't have any money saved. They didn't pay us in the summer. So your last paycheck in June, you got the next paycheck around, full paycheck around third week in September … So to not have a paycheck from June to November, or whatever … I mean, I saved money as best I could. But it was painful for me in terms of the climate that it created in the school between professionals. Well, you know, if you crossed or anybody crossed, you were forever a scab. And they treated you that way. So the first strike—if they're short, most people will try to the best of their ability. But the strike that went on for two months, there were people that just couldn't stay out any longer, short of being homeless and whatnot, including myself.[12]

> I found out right before that strike happened, so it had to be in '73 because my second child was born in '73, that I was pregnant. And I told everyone, *You can hate me if you want, but* … back in those days, you didn't get paid when you were out on maternity leave, and I said, *Look, I have a home and two cars and a child on the way. I am sorry, but I am gonna work.* So, I mean there were people that never spoke to me again for working.[13]

In addition to the financial cost of striking, not striking and going into schools to work threatened Black educators' collegial relationships both during

---

12   Interview, July 29, 2010.
13   Interview, June 21, 2010.

the strikes and for years after. During the strikes, Black educators heard Black strikebreakers taunted by picketers with the terms "scab," "uppity niggers," and "handkerchief heads."[14] They did not expect to be assaulted by racial epithets, as their colleagues had never used these words in general interracial conversations. However, during strike times, racial slurs were used as weapons against Black educators who did not side with striking union members. The racist notions White strikers had for Blacks had been hidden and surfaced during these tumultuous times. After the strikes, when educators returned to work, the ill feelings aroused during the strikes lingered for decades.

Racial issues were exacerbated by this series of strikes within SDP in the 1970s and 1980s. When the strikes ended, Black educators generally let bygones be bygones intraracially. However, collegial interactions between Black educators and White colleagues who went on strike were forever marred in some cases.

I don't know Black folks that fell out over the strikes. So, some people crossed and some people didn't. But they weren't falling out about it. Okay, but there were White folks who fell out with Black folks. And then these Black people, like at Strawberry Mansion, there was, there weren't any White people who crossed the picket lines. The only folks who crossed the lines were Black. And, for the rest of the year, they would go to their mailboxes and there'd be glue in their mailboxes. Just really sophomoric kinds of things. They tried to torture [them] for the rest of the year. They wouldn't speak to them. I can remember when I got to Mansion, a woman who had crossed the line and she had been teaching for 30 years. They wouldn't give her a retirement party ... I remember we ended up having something at like a club, just something really small. And it was my first year at Strawberry Mansion. And I really didn't know that lady, but she had been teaching 30 years, and I said, *You know what? No. I don't care how many lines she crossed. We don't do this.* So, it really divided. It was really unfortunate. Because some of those people had really been colleagues. It divided progressives, White union folks from Black people who, at the end of the day some of them were like *Yeah, I gotta pay my bills.* And others of them really felt like *These are our kids* and they really felt that that was the best way. And then it created this thing where the kids felt very protective of those teachers who crossed the picket lines. Because they identified them as teachers who really cared about them. So it was really, that was really a horrible, horrible strike that I believe it took years to recover from. That was in the early eighties.[15]

---

14 Interview, June 28, 2010; Interview, July 12, 2010; Interview, July 15, 2010; Interview, July 26, 2010; Interview, July 29, 2010.
15 Interview, July 12, 2010.

The multiple ways in which these narrators approached the teacher strikes demonstrates Black educators' resilience as they navigated relationships with colleagues and students, and supported their communities when district policies or professional practices seem counterintuitive and counterproductive. The impact of SDP's reforms on Black educators was based on their individual professional trajectory. Constant reforms can make educators weary, especially if those educators have significant historical knowledge and institutional memory. The professional situations of Black educators were influenced by the policies, practices, and politics of the school and school district in which these educators work. Interpretations of district reform policies combined with educators' efficacy and job situation, and the sums of these combinations became these educators' definitions of their professional situation. Here are the choices they made regarding whether to stay or to go: they waited for reforms' glory to pass until something or some new superintendent came along; they remained in the district until retirement; they left SDP to work in a charter school; or they left SDP to work for a suburban district. With the current proliferation of charter management organizations, while SDP closes schools and lays off educators, Black educators continue to be resilient, while remaining vulnerable.

REFERENCES

Agee, J. (2004). Negotiating a teaching identity: An African American teacher's struggle to teach in test-driven contexts. *Teachers College Record, 106*(4), 747–774.

Allen, K., Jacobson, S., & Lomotey, K. (1995). African American women in educational administration: The importance of mentors and sponsors. *The Journal of Negro Education, 64*(4), 409–422.

Aronson, J. (2004). The threat of stereotype. *Educational Leadership, 62*(3), 14–20.

Anyon, J. (2005). *Radical possibilities*. New York: Routledge.

Beauboeuf-Lafontant, T. (2002). A womanist experience of caring: Understanding the pedagogy of exemplary black women teachers. *Urban Review, 34*(1), 71–86.

Berger, P. L., & Luckmann, T. (1967). *The social construction of reality: A treatise in the sociology of knowledge*. New York: Anchor.

Birger, J. (1996). Race, reaction, and reform: The three Rs of Philadelphia school politics, 1965–1971. *The Pennsylvania Magazine of History and Biography, 120*(3), 163–216.

Bobek, B. L. (2002). Teacher resiliency: A key to career longevity. *The Clearing House, 75*(4), 202–205.

Bruner, J. (1991). The narrative construction of reality. *Critical Inquiry, 18*(1), 1–21.

Bruner, J. (1998). What is narrative fact? *Annals of the American Academy of Political and Social Science, 560*, 17–27.

Countryman, M. J. (2006). *Up South*. Philadelphia, PA: University of Pennsylvania Press.

Cuban, L., & Usdan, M. (Eds.) (2003). *Powerful reforms with shallow roots: Improving America's urban schools*. New York: Teachers College Press.

Dean, M. M. (2008, September 10). Black teachers in Phila. Schools: A vanishing breed. *Philadelphia Daily News*.

Delpit, L. (1995). *Other people's children: Cultural conflicts in the classroom*. New York: The New Press.

Dingus, J. E. (2006). "Doing the best we could": African American teachers' counterstory on school desegregation. *The Urban Review, 38*(3), 211–233.

Dixson, A. D., Royal, C., & Henry, K. L. (2014). School reform and school choice. In H. Richard Milner & Kofi Lomotey (Eds.), *Handbook of urban education*. New York: Routledge.

Dworkin, A. G. (2001). Perspective on teacher burnout and school reform. *International Education Journal, 2*(2), 69–79.

Foster, M. (1990). The politics of race: Through the eyes of African-American teachers. *Journal of Education, 172*, 123–141.

Foster, M. (1991). Constancy, connectedness, and constraints in the lives of African-American teachers. *NWSA Journal, 3*(2), 233–261.

Foster, M. (1997). *Black teachers on teaching*. New York: The New Press.

Franklin, V. P. (1979). *The education of Black Philadelphia: The social and educational history of a minority community, 1900–1950*. Philadelphia, PA: University of Pennsylvania.

Gordon, J. (2000). *The color of teaching*. New York: Routledge-Farmer.

Hargreaves, A. (1996). Revisiting voice. *Educational Researcher, 25*, 12–19.

Hayre, R. W., & Moore, A. (1997). *Tell them we are rising: A memoir of faith in education*. New York: John Wiley & Sons.

Ingersoll, R. (2001). *Teacher turnover, teacher shortages, and the organization of schools*. Seattle, WA: Center for the Study of Teaching and Policy.

Ingersoll, R. (2003). *Who controls teachers' work?: Power and accountability in America's schools*. Cambridge, MA: Harvard University Press.

Irvine, J. (1989). Beyond role models: An examination of cultural influences on the pedagogical perspectives of Black teachers. *Peabody Journal of Education, 66*(4), 51–63.

Jones, B. A. (2005). Forces for failure and genocide: The plantation model of urban educational policy making in St. Louis. *Educational Studies, 37*(1), 6–24.

Jones, C. (2002). Teachers' perceptions of African American principals' leadership in urban schools. *Peabody Journal of Education, 77*(1), 7–34.

Kelly, H. (2007). Racial tokenism in the school workplace: An exploratory study of Black teachers in overwhelmingly White schools. *Educational Studies, 41*(3), 230–254.

Kozol, J. (1991). *Savage inequalities*. New York: Harper Perennial.

Ladson-Billings, G. (1994). *Dreamkeepers: Successful teachers of African-American children*. New York: Jossey-Bass.

Ladson-Billings, G., & Tate, W. F. (1995). Toward a critical race theory of education. *Teachers College Record, 97*(1), 47–68.

Lynn, M. (2006). Race, culture, and the education of African Americans. *Educational Theory, 56*(1), 107–119.

Mac Iver, M. A., & Vaughn, E. S. (2007). "But how long will they stay?" Alternative certification and new teacher retention in an urban district. *Educational Research Service Spectrum, 25*(2), 33–44.

Matsuda, M., Lawrence, C., Delgado, R., & Crenshaw, K. (Eds.) (1993). *Words that wound: Critical race theory, assaultive speech, and the First Amendment*. Boulder, CO: Westview.

Milner, H. R., & Hoy, A. W. (2003). A case study of an African American teacher's self-efficacy, stereotype threat, and persistence. *Teaching and Teacher Education, 19*(2), 263–276.

Moore, C. M. (2012). The role of school environment in teacher dissatisfaction among U.S. public school teachers. *SAGE Open*, 1–16.

Murrell, P. C. (2000). Community teachers: A conceptual framework for preparing exemplary urban teachers. *Journal of Negro Education, 69*(4), 338–348.

Neild, R., Useem, E., & Farley, E. (2005). *The quest for quality: Recruiting and retaining teachers in Philadelphia*. Philadelphia, PA: Research for Action.

Neild, R. C., Useem, E., Travers, E. F., & Lesnick, J. (2003). *Once and for all: Placing a highly qualified teacher in every Philadelphia classroom*. Philadelphia, PA: Research for Action.

Nieto, S. (2003). *What keeps teachers going?* New York: Teachers College Press.

Noguera, P. (2003). *City schools and the American dream*. New York: Teachers College Press.

Oates, G. (2003). Teacher–student racial congruence, teacher perceptions, and test performance. *Social Science Quarterly, 84*(3), 508–525.

Patterson, J. H., Collins, L., & Abbott, G. (2004). A study of teacher resilience in urban schools. *Journal of Instructional Psychology, 31*(1), 3–11.

Phillips, A. E. (2005). A history of the struggle for school desegregation in Philadelphia, 1955–1967. *Pennsylvania History: A Journal of Mid-Atlantic Studies, 72*(1), 49–76.

Rex, L. A., & Nelson, M. C. (2004). How Teachers' professional identities position high-stakes test preparation in their classrooms. *Teachers College Record, 106*(6), 1299–1331.

Royal, C. (2009, April). *Reflections of three Black Philadelphia educators: An oral history*. Unpublished paper presented at the Annual Meeting of the American Educational Research Association, Division F, History and Historiography, San Diego, CA.

Royal, C. (2012). *Policies, politics, and protests: Black educators and the shifting landscape of Philadelphia's school reforms, 1967–2007* (Unpublished dissertation). Temple University, Philadelphia.

Royal, C., & Gibson, S. (in press). "They schools": Culturally relevant pedagogy under siege. *Teachers College Record* [special issue on culturally relevant pedagogy].

Stanford, G. C. (1997). Successful pedagogy in urban schools: Perspectives of four African American teachers. *Journal of Education for Students Placed at Risk, 2*(2), 107–119.

Taylor, E. (2006). A critical race analysis of the achievement gap in the United States: Politics, reality, and hope. *Leadership and Policy in Schools, 5*(1), 71–87.

Tyack, D., & Cuban, L. (1995). *Tinkering toward utopia: A century of public school reform*. Cambridge, MA: Harvard University Press.

Useem, E., Christman, J. B., & Boyd, W. L. (2006). *The role of district leadership in radical reform: Philadelphia's experience under the state takeover, 2001–2006*. Philadelphia, PA: Research for Action.

Useem, E., Offenberg, R., & Farley, E. (2007). *Closing the teacher quality gap in Philadelphia: New hope and old hurdles*. Philadelphia, PA: Research for Action.

Vila, P. (2000). Appendix: Categories, interpellations, metaphors and narratives: A brief theoretical discussion. In *Crossing borders, reinforcing borders: Social categories, metaphors and narrative identities on the U.S.-Mexico frontier* (pp. 227–249). Austin, TX: University of Texas Press.

Weiner, L. (1999). To teach or not to teach in an urban school? *English Journal, 88*(5), 21–25.

Wilms, W. W. (2003). Altering the structure and culture of American public schools. *Phi Delta Kappan, 84*(8), 606–615.

Wong, K. K., & Shen, F. X. (2003). Big city mayors and school governance reform: The case of school district takeover. *Peabody Journal of Education, 78*(1), 5–32.

8 Promoting culturally responsive practice to reduce disparities in school discipline among African American students

Katrina J. Debnam, Jessika H. Bottiani, and Catherine P. Bradshaw

Disproportionate representation, or disproportionality, refers to the over- or underrepresentation of a given population group in a specific category; it is often defined by racial and ethnic backgrounds, but also defined by socio-economic status, national origin, English proficiency, gender, and sexual orientation (Elementary & Middle Schools Technical Assistance Center, 2015). Disproportionality occurs across a number of areas and fields, including health, education, and employment. For example, the overrepresentation of minorities in adverse health outcomes is often referred to as health disparities (Carter-Pokras & Baquet, 2002). There is also documented underrepresentation of women and ethnic minorities in science, technology, engineering, and math fields (Linn, 2007). In education, disproportionate outcomes for African American youth have been observed fairly consistently in special education placement (e.g., mental retardation, severe emotional disturbance) (Artiles, Kozleski, Trent, Osher, & Ortiz, 2010; Donovan & Cross, 2002; Morgan, Salomon, Plotkin, & Cohen, 2014; Skiba et al., 2011) and school discipline practices, including office disciplinary referrals (ODRs) (Bradshaw, Mitchell, O'Brennan, & Leaf, 2010; Skiba et al., 2008, 2011), suspensions (Krezmien, Leone, & Achilles, 2006; Mendez & Knoff, 2003; Porowski, O'Conner, & Passa, 2014), and expulsions (Porowski et al., 2014; Wallace, Goodkind, Wallace, & Bachman, 2008).

Historically, national discourse on disproportionality in educational outcomes has most often focused on disparities in special education placement or academic achievement between White and African American students. However, recent evidence suggests an even greater need to understand and address disproportionality in school discipline practices. Here disproportionality is defined as the over- or underrepresentation of a particular population or demographic group in discipline data relative to the presence of this group in the overall student population (National Association for Bilingual Education, 2002). In this chapter, we first review the national data available on disproportionality in school discipline and the long-term impact of disciplinary contact for African American youth. We then consider the historical context of policies and procedures that have contributed to the current data and review the existing research in this area. Finally, we offer an overview of a promising framework, Double Check, which stresses strengthening school staff culturally responsive practice to address this problem. Although our focus in this book and chapter is African American students, similar disparities in school discipline exist for Latino and American Indian students. It is likely that any comprehensive intervention that addresses school staff's culturally responsive practice will also positively impact Latino and American Indian students.

DISPROPORTIONALITY IN SCHOOL DISCIPLINE

Collectively, office discipline referrals, suspensions, and expulsions are considered *exclusionary* discipline, because the disciplinary strategies remove and exclude students from schools (and classroom learning time) as a punitive consequence to an infraction of school or classroom rules or expectations. Disproportionality occurs as a result of the subjective nature of school discipline, meaning the behavioral definitions of infractions, and consequences imposed, vary widely within and across schools. Some types of student infractions can be considered more objective, such as graffiti, smoking on school grounds, or carrying a weapon to school; they are objective in that a student either did or did not commit these violations—there is not much room for interpretation (Skiba, Michael, Nardo, & Peterson, 2002). Other infractions can be understood as subjective, also called "soft" offenses, which include defiance, insubordination, and disrespect; these types of offenses rely relatively more on school staff perceptions of students' behavior. Studies have found that White students typically receive suspensions for objective violations, whereas African American youth tend to receive suspensions for more subjective offenses (Skiba et al., 2008).

Studies examining demographic correlates of school discipline exposure overwhelmingly have found that African American students receive office discipline referrals, suspensions, and expulsions at higher rates than White students (Krezmien et al., 2006; Skiba et al., 2011; Vincent, Swain-Bradway, Tobin, & May, 2011; Wallace et al., 2008), even after controlling for the level of behavior problems (Bradshaw et al., 2010). National data from 2011–2012 show that African American students represent approximately 16% of the student population, but represent 32% to 42% of the students suspended or expelled (U.S. Department of Education, Office for Civil Rights, 2014). In comparison, White students also represent a similar range of between 31% and 40% of students suspended or expelled, but they are 51% of the student population (U.S. Department of Education, Office for Civil Rights, 2014). African American youth are not only punished with greater frequency, but also greater severity, with research finding harsher punishments (i.e., higher average number of days of suspension) for similar violations of school rules (Skiba et al., 2002). Even when given the opportunity to choose from several disciplinary options for a minor offense, school staff members often use more severe punishments for African American students than White students for the same offense (Rudd, 2014).

Unfortunately, this problem has only become worse over time. Specifically, as shown in Figure 8.1, national data from the U.S. Department of Education, Office of Civil Rights suggest the risk of out-of-school suspension has increased slightly over the past several decades for almost all racial ethnic groups, with the exception of African American youth. Among African American youth, represented here by the solid black line, the risk was already double that of White youth in 1973. Here, we see a sharply increasing trend, resulting in a risk of suspension among African American youth that quadruples that of White youth in 2012 (Losen, Hodson, Keith, Morrison, & Belway, 2015). These trends are quite troubling, considering the decades of educational reform and increased emphasis on professional development focused on trying to reduce such disparities (Artiles et al., 2010). However, more recent estimates from the Office for Civil Rights suggest some tapering of this trend, which may reflect the impact of programmatic and policy interventions to mitigate the discipline gap.

Sex, disability, and socioeconomic (SES) status can also amplify disparities. African American males were found to be 16 times as likely as White females to be suspended (Gregory, 1997). Crenshaw, Ocen, and Nanda (2015) found that 90% of all females expelled from New York City schools in 2011–2012 were African American. Similarly, national data shows that African American females are suspended 6 times as often as their White counterparts (U.S. Department of Education Office for Civil Rights, 2014). Given that African American students are also overrepresented in special education, it is not surprising that students with a disability are more than twice as likely to receive an out-of-school suspension (13%) than students without

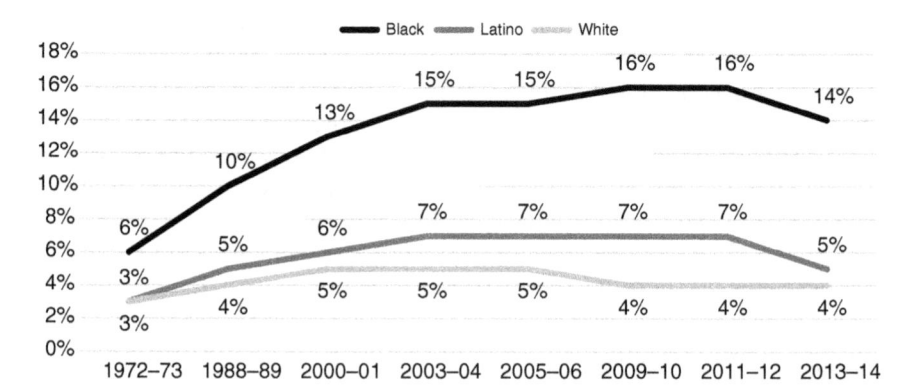

Figure 8.1 Kindergarten to 12th grade suspension rates by race/ethnicity and year. (Data from Children's Defense Fund, 1975 [1972–1973 school year]; Losen et al., 2015 [1988–1989 school year]; and U.S. Department of Education, Office for Civil Rights [2000–2014].)

disabilities (6%). Moreover, a study examining the cumulative impact of race, sex, and disability found that more than 1 out of 4 boys of color with disabilities and nearly 1 in 5 girls of color with disabilities receives an out-of-school suspension (U.S. Department of Education, Office for Civil Rights, 2014). Finally, poverty has been shown to be a consistent predictor of school discipline; Petras, Masyn, Buckley, Ialongo, and Sheppard (2011) found that students who live in poverty were more likely to be removed from school after controlling for similar levels of aggression among students.

Although it may be argued that SES is the hidden contributor to disproportionality in race and ethnicity due to a high correlation between race and SES, research consistently finds that student SES is limited in its ability to explain disproportionate disciplinary contact. For example, Wallace et al. (2008) found that race and ethnicity remained a significant predictor of office disciplinary referrals, suspensions, and expulsions after accounting for parental education, family structure, and urbanicity of neighborhood. Thus, though being from a low-income neighborhood may increase the likelihood of experiencing punitive school discipline, student SES is not sufficient to explain disproportionate rates. Regardless of your view of the role of SES, with so many African American students impacted by exclusionary discipline practices, it is important to examine what short- and long-term effects these practices have on the outcomes of students.

ACADEMIC, HEALTH, AND SOCIETAL CONSEQUENCES OF EXCLUSIONARY DISCIPLINE

The harmful effects of the exclusionary discipline that disproportionately affects African American youth are substantial. A life-course developmental perspective (Elder, 1998) highlights how early gaps in academic learning can incrementally alter developmental trajectories, contributing to health and economic disparities over the life course (Dankwa-Mullan et al., 2010). Disparities in educational pathways in the transition to adulthood especially merit research attention, as academic failure and school dropout in high school are well-documented determinants of adult health outcomes (Harper & Lynch, 2007). Here we detail the academic (e.g., grade retention, dropout, and postsecondary opportunities), health (e.g., disengagement, substance use), and societal (e.g., juvenile justice and prison) consequences of exclusionary discipline practices on African American youth.

Academic consequences

Decades of research show that increasing opportunities for student learning is associated with greater academic achievement (Rausch, Skiba, & Simmons, 2004). Thus, you can imagine what may happen to students whose learning time is thwarted by office disciplinary referrals and discipline practices. Indeed, a study in an urban elementary school found that suspended students lost 202.7 hours of class time due to office referrals and 462 hours of class time due to suspensions (Scott & Barrett, 2004). With this significant loss of learning time, it is not surprising that students who are suspended or expelled are twice as likely to repeat their grade when compared to students with their same demographic characteristics who attend a similar school and who had not been suspended or expelled (Fabelo et al., 2011). Being suspended is also associated with a greater likelihood of recurring misbehavior and future suspension (Anfinson, Autumn, Lehr, Riestenberg, & Scullin, 2010). Finally, the *Breaking School Rules Report* (Fabelo et al., 2011), a landmark statewide study of juvenile records in Texas, found that about 10% of students suspended or expelled between 7th and 12th grade dropped out of school. Another study found that if a student receives a suspension in 9th grade, each additional suspension further decreases their odds of graduating high school by 20% and decreases their odds of enrolling in postsecondary school by 12% (Balfanz, Byrnes, & Fox, 2012).

Health consequences

Students who receive exclusionary discipline practices often report greater levels of academic disengagement and negative perceptions of school compared to their peers who are not receiving school discipline (Brown, 2007; Moreno & Gaytán, 2012). In addition, Brown (2007) showed that high-suspension students were less likely than low-suspension students to report good relationships with both teachers and administrators. Brown's study of students attending an urban public alternative high school also reported that only a very small percentage of participating students felt that adults were "very concerned" about their well-being. The compounded impact of losing learning time and feeling less connected with teachers and school are likely large contributing factors to the reported rates of grade retention and school dropout among students receiving suspensions.

Moreover, research shows that students who are out of school due to exclusionary discipline are more likely to engage in other risky health behaviors. For example, a recent study with grade 7 and 9 students showed that school suspension remained a predictor of current tobacco use after controlling for other established risk factors including prior tobacco and other drug use (Hemphill, Heerde, Herrenkohl, Toumbourou, & Catalano, 2012). MacLean, Kutin, Best, Bruun, and Green (2014) found that in a sample of youth who had used drugs at least once in the past 6 months, 83% of them also reported they had been suspended from school or an educational program at some point during their adolescence. Finally, Fortunato, Young, Boyd, and Fons (2010) saw significant associations between exclusionary discipline (i.e., detentions and suspensions) and risky sexual behaviors among urban middle and high school students.

Societal consequences

With a life-course developmental perspective in mind, exclusionary school discipline practices are a key component of the policies and procedures that push students out of the classroom and into the criminal justice system at alarming rates (i.e., school-to-prison pipeline). For example, having been suspended or expelled or dropping out of school is strongly related to juvenile delinquency (Forsyth et al., 2013). Again, the *Breaking School Rules Report* (Fabelo et al., 2011) found that of students disciplined in middle or high school, 23% of them ended up in contact with a juvenile probation officer compared to just 2% of students who had no school disciplinary actions. Overall, 20% of African American students were in contact with the juvenile justice system during the study, in contrast to 17% Hispanic and 11% White students. In considering male students, 26% of African American males, compared to 22% Hispanic and 14% White male students, had contact with the juvenile justice system. A similar trend occurs for females, such that 14% of African American females and 13% of Hispanic females had contact with the juvenile justice system, as compared to 8% of White females. Furthermore, the likelihood of coming into contact with the juvenile justice system increases with the number of suspensions experienced. Almost half of students (46%) who had a "high" number of disciplinary contacts (11 or more sanctions) were in contact with the juvenile justice system. Similar results were reported in a study by Monahan, VanDerhei, Bechtold, and Cauffman (2014), who found that being suspended or expelled from school increased the likelihood of arrest in that same month. Although office referrals and school suspensions are not the only factors (e.g., structural racism [Smith, 2009], zero tolerance policies [Skiba & Knesting, 2001], school climate [Christle, Jolivette, & Nelson, 2005], and teacher education [Raible & Irizarry, 2010]) contributing to the school-to-prison pipeline, it is clear that more preventive efforts are needed in schools and classrooms to stem this trend.

NATIONAL INITIATIVES

Although the first major national report calling attention to the discipline gap was released four decades ago in 1975, national policy initiatives to stem school discipline disparities and the school-to-prison pipeline have only emerged in recent years, following decades of national policy efforts to end educational inequities within achievement and special education (Aud et al., 2011; Donovan & Cross, 2002). Gains have also been made in recent years in relation to the reduced use of zero tolerance initiatives. In fact, the increasing rates of exclusionary discipline across all demographic groups likely have been exacerbated by the growing use of zero tolerance initiatives, which place strict and rigidly applied penalties on even minor rule violations without regard to context in which the violation occurred or the student's history. Many schools and districts adopted these policies in full force during an era of fear and distress for school safety following the Columbine High School massacre in 1999, as shown in Figure 8.2. However, there has been a shift in the momentum for school zero tolerance policies as many major professional organizations have come out against schools' application of zero tolerance policies. For example, the American Bar Association in 2001 and the American Psychological Association in 2008 both cited a number of concerns regarding the disproportionate impact of these types of policies on students of color. The number of such reports and objections to zero tolerance policies has increased in recent years, with many citing it as a factor contributing to the discipline gap and the school-to-prison pipeline. As a result, some substantial policy changes countering zero tolerance have occurred in vanguard districts like New York City Department of Education and Los Angeles Unified School District. In 2014, Maryland overturned its zero tolerance policy, impacting all 24 school districts in the state. It is expected that other major urban districts and states may follow suit in coming years.

The Obama administration's Race to the Top initiative, launched in 2009, required that grantees demonstrating discipline disproportionality conduct a root cause analysis and develop an action plan to redress the problem as a prerequisite of receiving funding through the program. In 2011, the U.S. Departments of Education and Justice began coordinating efforts through a new endeavor called the Supportive School Discipline Initiative (SSDI) to promote the use of more positive, supportive, and restorative discipline practices and to stem the tide of zero tolerance policies. The SSDI initiative released joint recommendations for ending discriminatory discipline practices in schools in June 2014 that highlighted the importance of targeted behavioral interventions and school–police partnerships.

President Obama's My Brother's Keeper initiative also aimed to address the discipline gap by building "ladders of opportunity" for boys and young men of color, and lends new urgency to addressing the problem of disparate educational, health, and economic outcomes of men of color in particular (White House, Office of Press Secretary, 2014). Released in February 2014, the president's initiative encourages communities (including schools) to develop innovative strategies and practices to improve outcomes for boys and young men of color by "keeping kids on track and giving them second chances." Work is underway at the national level to provide more concrete and detailed plans for this initiative.

RESEARCH INITIATIVES

As noted earlier, extensive research has been conducted to document the discipline gap. This research continues to grow, particularly as the U.S. Department of Education's Office of Civil Rights has reinvigorated its Civil Rights data collection, which requires schools nationally to report on their

1975

Children's Defense Fund releases national report "School Suspensions: Are They Helping Our Children?" that highlights racial disparities in school discipline practices for African American students—September 1, 1975

1999

Zero tolerance policies flourish following **Columbine High School Massacre**—April 20, 1999

2001

American Bar Association opposes zero tolerance policies that mandate either expulsion or referral of students to juvenile or criminal court, without regard to the circumstances or nature of the offense or the student's history—February 2001

2008

American Psychological Association's **Zero Tolerance Task Force** finds zero tolerance policies ineffective, harmful, disproportionately affect students of color—December 2008

2009

Obama Administration launches the **Race to the Top Initiative** requiring that grant recipients with racially disproportionate discipline practices conduct root cause analysis and develop action plan to remediate problem—July 25, 2009

2011

National report **"Federal Policy, ESEA Reauthorization, and the School-to-Prison Pipeline"** endorsed by 150 organizations—March 2011

The Civil Rights Project at UCLA opens the **Center for Civil Rights Remedies** led by Dan Losen and focused explicitly on the school discipline gap—July 2011

Attorney General Eric Holder and Secretary of Education Arne Duncan announce the launch of the **Supportive School Discipline Initiative**, a collaborative project of the Departments of Justice and Education to address the school-to-prison pipeline—July 21, 2011

Center for State Government's Justice Policy Center releases **Breaking School Rules report** which linked exposure to suspensions to subsequent juvenile justice system contact—July 2011

Figure 8.2 The discipline gap: A timeline. *(Continued)*

suspensions and expulsions by race, ethnicity, gender, and disability status. There is also research highlighting best practice and evidence-based practices for reducing suspension rates overall, which was underscored in the joint report by the Departments of Education and Justice in the *School Discipline Consensus Project*.

Yet a recent systematic review of the literature suggests that there is little empirical research examining the impact of school-based interventions to promote school and teacher culturally responsive practice (Bottiani, Larson,

2013

The Center for Civil Rights Remedies holds the **"Closing the School Discipline Gap" national conference** bringing together scholars, practitioners, and advocates to discuss potential solutions—January 2013

Los Angeles Unified School District bans suspensions for "willful defiance"—May 14, 2013

2014

Maryland School Board overturns zero tolerance policy across 24 districts January 28, 2014

The Obama Administration launches the **My Brother's Keeper** Initiative which encourages communities to develop innovative strategies and practices to improve outcomes for boys and young men of color by "keeping kids on track and giving them second chances—February 27, 2014

The **Discipline Disparities Research-to-Practice Collaborative** at Indiana University (Russ Skiba) releases series of national reports on discipline gap—March 13, 2014

U.S. Department of Education's **Institute of Education Sciences releases report** "Disproportionality in school discipline: An assessment of trends in Maryland"—March 5, 2014

Council of State Governments Justice Center (CSG Justice Center) releases the **School Discipline Consensus Report**, U.S. Departments of Education and Justice's joint recommendations for ending discriminatory school discipline policies—June 3, 2014

2015

New York City Department of Education calls for an end to principal-led suspensions— February 2015

The Center for Civil Rights Remedies releases major national report **"Are We Closing the School Discipline Gap?"**—February 13, 2015

U.S. Department of Education's **Office of Civil Rights reinvigorates data collection**, receives OMB approval to require every public school and school district in the country to respond to the 2013-14 Civil Rights Data Collection, which collects suspension and expulsion data by race, disability, and gender—April 9, 2015

The Center for the Study of Race and Equity at the University of Pennsylvania releases **report highlighting dramatic gaps in the U.S. South**—August 2015

Black Lives Matter movement growing in education sector—September 2015

Figure 8.2 (Continued) The discipline gap: A timeline.

Debnam, Bischoff, & Bradshaw, 2015). The review applied a systematic search, study selection, and quality analysis process, employing systematic review methods recommended by the Campbell Collaborative (Hammerstrøm, Wade, & Jørgensen, 2010). The findings suggest a substantial lack of outcome-focused research assessing the effectiveness of such in-service interventions. Specifically, of the 179 unduplicated articles yielded from the basic search, only 10 articles reported on an empirical examination of the impact of a culturally responsive practice in-service intervention. None of the 10 articles met rigorous standards of evidence to establish efficacy of the intervention (Flay et al., 2005; Gottfredson et al., 2015), with the majority of studies being qualitative impact assessments. The central finding of the review highlights the need to strengthen empirical research examining whether in-service intervention to support teachers' and administrators' culturally responsive practices translate to improvements in the use of culturally responsive practices in schools (e.g., responsive interactions with students, classroom structure, instructional materials), as well as equity and improvement in student academic, social, emotional, and disciplinary outcomes. Aside from inadequate study designs, an important factor hindering research progress to support evidence-based culturally responsive practice is the lack of consistent, integrated, psychometrically sound measurement approaches. The review findings also highlight the need for more rigorous research approaches to identify which culturally responsive practice in-service interventions are effective and therefore could be disseminated and brought to scale to ensure equitable, high-quality learning environments for all students.

Although disheartening, the findings from the Bottiani et al. (2015) study were not surprising, given the numerous conceptual, methodological, and practical complexities associated with conducting research on culturally responsive practices. In fact, there is a lack of consensus in the field about how to operationalize and measure culturally responsive practice. For example, self-report of culturally responsive practice has consistently been found to correlate highly with measures of social desirability bias (Larson & Bradshaw, 2015), suggesting teachers tend to overestimate their use of culturally responsive practices. Moreover, it is difficult to conduct experimental and longitudinal research on these types of sensitive issues and the use of different types of disciplinary practices. However, the increasing culturally, racially, and ethnically diverse landscape of teaching and learning highlights the growing need for quality empirical research on culturally responsive practices to support equity and excellence.

A PROMISING FRAMEWORK TO IMPROVE CULTURALLY RESPONSIVE PRACTICE

One prevention framework for which there is emerging research to suggest it may be effective at reducing rates of office referrals and suspension is Positive Behavioral Interventions and Supports (PBIS). PBIS emphasizes comprehensive, data-driven, incremental intervention in schools (Sugai et al., 2000) to improve school climate and reduce discipline problems. School climate includes domains related to emotional and physical safety, supportive relationships, and an engaging learning environment. PBIS is premised upon the public health preventive intervention and mental health promotion framework (Mrazek & Haggerty, 1994; O'Connell, Boat, & Warner, 2009) in which universal, selective, and indicated preventive interventions are delivered through a multitiered system of supports. Although PBIS has demonstrated success in improving school climate and reducing office disciplinary referral rates overall (Bradshaw, Koth, Thornton, & Leaf, 2009; Horner et al., 2009), a number of studies have documented that racial disparities in school discipline practices affecting African American students remained relatively unchanged in schools implementing schoolwide PBIS (Bradshaw et al., 2010; Kaufman et al., 2010; Vincent, Randall, Cartledge, Tobin, & Swain-Bradway, 2011).

Recognizing this gap, the Double Check framework was designed to build upon PBIS to promote and sustain culturally responsive practice (Bradshaw & Rosenberg, in press). Through professional development and individualized coaching, Double Check facilitates the recognition of cultural inconsistencies in behavior management practices and facilitates the development of actionable culturally responsive practices that can result in a reduction in exclusionary discipline and improvements in student engagement and academic achievement. Double Check is comprised of five specific domains (described in the following sections), collectively referred to as Double Check CARES, each with its own set of outcomes, application activities, and supports for sustainability and success (Bradshaw & Rosenberg, in press; Rosenberg, Westling, & McLeskey, 2011). Taken together, the intended outcome is for schools to apply the elements of the domains to enhance culturally responsive practices, ultimately reducing instances of disproportional disciplinary referrals for African American students.

Connection to the curriculum

Connection to the curriculum refers to tangibly linking all elements of lesson planning and classroom instruction to students' cultural backgrounds. This connection must go beyond the superficiality of *heroes and holidays* and focus on the delivery of learning activities that resonate well below the surface of observable traditions and artistic expressions. Visible images reflecting cultural value should be on display and learning activities should be developed or selected with a keen eye toward students' backgrounds, values, families, and communities. Moreover, it is essential that the prevailing attitude guiding curriculum and instruction reflect a partnership between teacher and student in the goal of mastering the material (Gay, 2002; Haberman, 1995; McIntyre, 1996; Ross, Kamman, & Coady, 2008).

Authentic relationships

Authentic relationships between educators and students are characterized by tangible evidence of warmth, caring, and trust. These types of relationships take time to develop and typically grow from brief interactions such as warm greetings upon entry to the classroom and intermittent expressions of interest in students' lives outside the classroom. These relationships evolve rapidly when educators reveal their enthusiasm, caring, values, and willingness to help students meet academic and behavioral challenges (McLeskey, Rosenberg, & Westling, 2013). Positive relationships between students and teachers help students adjust to the pressures of the classroom, promote social competence, and are associated with fewer behavior problems (Hamre & Pianta, 2001; McNeely, Nonnemaker, & Blum, 2002; Murray & Greenberg, 2001; Scott, Alter, Rosenberg, & Borgmeier, 2010). In addition to explicit expressions of warmth, caring, and trust, specific indicators of a teacher's initiating and sustaining positive relationships include: positive attention directed toward the student (e.g., recognizing special talents, encouragement during lessons, and the provision of emotional support); interest and participation in the student's activities and personal life; and truly listening to the student rather than just reacting to overt behavior (Koenig, 2000; Monroe, 2006a,b).

Reflective thinking

The reflective thinking domain of the Double Check framework relates to the examination of one's own social, cultural, and class membership, and how these factors interact with the group memberships of students. Indicators of thoughtful reflection related to culturally responsive practice include (1) understanding the concept of culture and why it is important; (2) being aware of one's own and others' sociocultural histories; (3) considering how past and current circumstances contribute to presenting behaviors; (4) examining one's own attitudes and biases, and seeing how they impact relationships with students; (5) articulating positive and constructive views of difference; and (6) making tangible efforts to reach out and understand differences (Richards, Brown, & Forde, 2007; Villegas & Lucas, 2002).

Effective communication

Effective communication within the Double Check framework refers to recognizing the distinct interactive styles of African American students and knowing how to respond to these differences with civility, respect, and high expectations. Indicators of effective culturally responsive communication style among educators include: (1) understanding the communicative function of the student's different types of behavior; (2) consistent evidence of interactions that reflect professionalism, credibility, civility, and respect; (3) limited judgmental verbal interactions directed toward the student; and (4) facility with *code-switching* and recognizing that some students may need guidance in knowing how varying contexts require different standards of behavior (Day-Vines & Day-Hairston, 2005; Gay, 2010; Richards et al., 2007).

Sensitivity to students' culture

Sensitivity to students' culture requires both (a) an understanding that some students present behaviors that are not always aligned with typical school expectations and (b) an acknowledgment that these behavioral differences are not deficits. Many students experience different patterns of behavior in their homes and communities, and are unable to fully comprehend the culture of their school and classrooms. Making connections with students' cultural community and family is an effective way to communicate a genuine desire to understand students' culture. For example, when families are included in classroom activities, teachers report a broadening of their own understanding of culture, and consequently, a richer understanding of their students. These connections also facilitate an understanding of the motivations for student behavior and have been found to reduce referrals for disciplinary problems (Epstein & Sheldon, 2002).

The Double Check framework was developed through a series of grants from the U.S. Department of Education Institute of Education Sciences and the Spencer Foundation. The broader framework can be implemented school-wide by building on schoolwide PBIS and include coaching for individual teachers and principals. The overall goal of Double Check is to promote educators' use of culturally responsive practices and to reduce disproportionate rates of disciplinary referrals for African American youth. Research is currently underway to determine the impact of the framework, as preliminary evidence suggests the model has promising impacts on teachers' use of culturally responsive behavior management and self-reports of efficacy.

CONCLUSION

The increasing use of school exclusion as a discipline strategy in the past several decades has disproportionately impacted African American children and youth, who presently are removed from school at 4 times the rate of their White peers. The developmental implications of excessive school exclusion for this population are far-reaching and likely further exacerbate longstanding racial disparities in adult health, economic, and justice outcomes. Empirically tested frameworks and interventions like PBIS and Double Check hold promise for reducing the long-term impacts of exclusionary discipline for African American youth.

REFERENCES

Anfinson, A., Autumn, S., Lehr, C., Riestenberg, N., & Scullin, S. (2010). Disproportionate minority representation in suspension and expulsion in Minnesota public schools. *International Journal on School Disaffection, 7*(2), 5–20. Retrieved from http://eric.ed.gov/?id=EJ970888

Artiles, A. J., Kozleski, E. B., Trent, S., Osher, D., & Ortiz, A. (2010). Justifying and explaining disproportionality, 1968–2008: A critique of underlying views of culture. *Exceptional Children, 76*(3), 279–299.

Aud, S., Hussar, W., Kena, G., Bianco, K., Frohlich, L., Kemp, J., & Tahan, K. (2011). *The Condition of Education 2011 (NCES 2011–033).* U.S. Department of Education, National Center for Education Statistics. Washington, DC: U.S. Government Printing Office.

Balfanz, R., Byrnes, V., & Fox, J. (2012). *Sent home and put off-track: The antecedents, disproportionalities, and consequences of being suspended in the ninth grade.* Center for Civil Rights Remedies and the Research-to-Practice Collaborative, National Conference on Race and Gender Disparities in Discipline, Johns Hopkins University. Retrieved from http://civilrightsproject.ucla.edu/resources/projects/center-for-civil-rights-remedies/school-to-prison-folder/state-reports/sent-home-and-put-off-track-the-antecedents-disproportionalities-and-consequences-of-being-suspended-in-the-ninth-grade/balfanz-sent-home-ccrr-conf-2013.pdf

Bottiani, J., Larson, K. E., Debnam, K. J., Bischoff, C., & Bradshaw, C. P. (2015). *Promoting educators' use of culturally responsive practices: A systematic review of in-service interventions.* Manuscript submitted for publication.

Bradshaw, C. P., Koth, C. W., Thornton, L. A., & Leaf, P. J. (2009). Altering school climate through school-wide Positive Behavioral Interventions and Supports: Findings from a group-randomized effectiveness trial. *Prevention Science, 10*(2), 100–115. doi:10.1007/s11121-008-0114-9

Bradshaw, C. P., Mitchell, M. M., O'Brennan, L. M., & Leaf, P. J. (2010). Multilevel exploration of factors contributing to the overrepresentation of Black students in office disciplinary referrals. *Journal of Educational Psychology, 102*(2), 508–520. http://dx.doi.org/10.1037/a0018450

Bradshaw, C. P., & Rosenberg, M. (in press). *Promoting culturally responsive behavior management.* New York: Guildford Press.

Brown, T. M. (2007). Lost and turned out: Academic, social, and emotional experiences of students excluded from school. *Urban Education, 42*(5), 432–455. doi:10.1177/0042085907304947

Carter-Pokras, O., & Baquet, C. (2002). What is a "health disparity"? *Public Health Report, 117*(5), 426–434.

Christle, C. A., Jolivette, K., & Nelson, C. M. (2005). Breaking the school to prison pipeline: Identifying school risk and protective factors for youth delinquency. *Exceptionality, 13*(2), 69–88.

Crenshaw, K. W., Ocen, P., & Nanda, J. (2015). *Black girls matter: Pushed out, over-policed, and underprotected.* New York: African American Policy Forum; Center for Intersectionality and Social Policy Studies. Retrieved from http://static1.squarespace.com/static/53f20d90e4b0b80451158d8c/t/54d2d37ce4b024b41443b0ba/1423102844010/BlackGirlsMatter_Report.pdf

Dankwa-Mullan, I., Rhee, K. B., Stoff, D. M., Pohlhaus, J. R., Sy, F. S., Stinson, N., Jr., & Ruffin, J. (2010). Moving toward paradigm-shifting research in health disparities through translational, transformational, and transdisciplinary approaches. *American Journal of Public Health, 100*(S1), S19–S24. doi:10.2105/ajph.2009.189167

Day-Vines, N., & Day-Hairston, B. (2005). Culturally congruent strategies for addressing the behavioral needs of urban, African American male adolescents. *Professional School Counseling, 8*(3), 236–243.

Donovan, M. S., & Cross, C. T. (Eds.). (2002). *Minority students in special and gifted education.* Washington, DC: National Academy Press.

Elder, G. H. (1998). The life course as developmental theory. *Child Development, 69*(1), 1–12. doi:10.1111/j.1467-8624.1998.tb06128.x

Elementary & Middle Schools Technical Assistance Center (EMSTAC). (2015). *Disproportionality: The disproportionate representation of racial and ethnic minorities in special education.* Retrieved from http://www.emstac.org/registered/topics/disproportionality/index.htm

Epstein, J. L., & Sheldon, S. B. (2002). Present and accounted for: Improving student attendance through family and community involvement. *Journal of Educational Research, 95*, 308–318.

Fabelo, T., Thompson, M. D., Plotkin, M., Carmichael, D., Marchbanks, M. P., III, & Booth, E. A. (2011). *Breaking schools' rules: A statewide study of how school discipline relates to students' success and juvenile justice involvement.* New York: Council of State Governments Justice Center. Retrieved from http://justicecenter .csg.org/files/Breaking_Schools_Rules_Report_Final.pdf

Flay, B. R., Biglan, A., Boruch, R. F., Gonzalez Castro, F., Gottfredson, D., Kellam, S., … Ji, P. (2005). Standards of evidence: Criteria for efficacy, effectiveness and dissemination. *Prevention Science, 6*(3), 151–175. doi:10.1007/s11121-005-5553-y

Forsyth, C. J., Howat, H., Pei, L. K., Forsyth, Y. A., Asmus, G., & Stokes, B. R. (2013). Examining the infractions causing higher rates of suspensions and expulsions: Racial and ethnic considerations. *Laws, 2*(1), 20–32.

Fortunato, L., Young, A. M., Boyd, C. J., & Fons, C. E. (2010). Hook-up sexual experiences and problem behaviors among adolescents. *Journal of Child & Adolescent Substance Abuse, 19*, 261–278. doi:10.1080/1067828X.2010.488965

Gay, G. (2002). Culturally responsive teaching in special education for ethnically diverse students: Setting the stage. *International Journal of Qualitative Studies in Education, 15*, 613–629.

Gay, G. (2010). *Culturally responsive teaching: Theory, research, and practice.* New York: Teachers College Press.

Gottfredson, D. C., Cook, T. D, Gardner, F., Gorman-Smith, D., Howe, G. W., Sandler, I. N., & Zafft, K. M. (2015). Standards of evidence for efficacy, effectiveness, and scale-up research in prevention science: Next generation. *Prevention Science, 16*(7), 893–926. doi:10.1007/s11121-015-0555-x

Gregory, J. F. (1997). Three strikes and they're out: African American boys and American schools' responses to misbehavior. *International Journal of Adolescence and Youth, 7*(1), 25–34.

Haberman, M. (1995). *Star teachers of children in poverty.* West Lafayette, IN: Kappa Delta Pi.

Hammerstrøm, K., Wade, A., & Jørgensen, A. (2010). *Searching for studies: A guide to information retrieval for Campbell Systematic Reviews.* Retrieved from http://www .campbellcollaboration.org/resources/research/new_information_retrieval_guide .php

Hamre, B. K., & Pianta, R. C. (2001). Early teacher-child relationships and the trajectory of children's school outcomes through eighth grade. *Child Development, 72*(2), 625–638. doi:10.1111/1467-8624.00301

Harper, S., & Lynch, J. (2007). Trends in socioeconomic inequalities in adult health behaviors among U.S. states, 1990–2004. *Public Health Reports, 122*(2), 177–198.

Hemphill, S. A., Heerde, J. A., Herrenkohl, T. I., Toumbourou, J. W., & Catalano, R. F. (2012). The impact of school suspension on student tobacco use: A longitudinal study in Victoria, Australia and Washington State, United States. *Health Education & Behavior: The Official Publication of the Society for Public Health Education, 39*(1), 45–56. http://doi.org/10.1177/1090198111406724

Horner, R. H., Sugai, G., Smolkowski, K., Eber, L., Nakasato, J., Todd, A. W., & Esperanza, J. (2009). A randomized, wait-list controlled effectiveness trial assessing school-wide positive behavior support in elementary schools. *Journal of Positive Behavior Interventions, 11*, 133–144. doi:10.1177/1098300709332067

Kaufman, J. S., Jaser, S. S., Vaughan, E. L., Reynolds, J. S., DiDonato, J., Bernard, S. N., & Hernandez-Brereton, M. (2010). Patterns in office discipline referral data by grade, race/ethnicity, and gender. *Journal of Positive Behavior Interventions, 12*, 44–54.

Koenig, L. (2000). *Smart discipline for the classroom: Respect and cooperation restored* (3rd ed.). Thousand Oaks, CA: Corwin.

Krezmien, M. P., Leone, P. E., & Achilles, G. M. (2006). Suspension, race, and disability: Analysis of statewide practices and reporting. *Journal of Emotional and Behavioral Disorders, 14*, 217–226. doi:10.1177/10634266060140040501

Larson, K., & Bradshaw, C. P. (2015). *Cultural competence and social desirability among practitioners and educators: A systematic review of the literature.* Manuscript submitted for publication.

Linn, M. (2007). Women in science: Can evidence inform the debate? *Science, 317,* 199–200.

Losen, D., Hodson, C., Keith, M. A., Morrison, K., & Belway, S. (2015). *Are we closing the school discipline gap?* The Center for Civil Rights Remedies at the Civil Rights Project at UCLA. Retrieved from http://civilrightsproject.ucla.edu/resources/projects/center-for-civil-rights-remedies/school-to-prison-folder/federal-reports/are-we-closing-the-school-discipline-gap/AreWeClosingTheSchoolDisciplineGap_FINAL221.pdf

MacLean, S. J., Kutin, J., Best, D., Bruun, A., & Green, R. (2014). Risk profiles for early adolescents who regularly use alcohol and other drugs compared with older youth, *Vulnerable Children and Youth Studies, 9*(1), 17–27. doi:10.1080/17450128.2012.750025

McIntyre, T. (1996). Does the way we teach create behavior disorders in culturally different students? *Education and Treatment of Children, 19*(3), 354–370.

McLeskey, J., Rosenberg, M. S, & Westling, D. L. (2013). *Inclusion: Effective practices for all students* (2nd ed.). New York: Pearson.

McNeely, C. A., Nonnemaker, J. M., & Blum, R. W. (2002). Promoting school connectedness: Evidence from the national longitudinal study of adolescent health. *Journal of School Health, 72*(4), 138–146. doi:10.1111/j.1746-1561.2002.tb06533.x

Mendez, L. M. R., & Knoff, H. M. (2003). Who gets suspended from school and why: A demographic analysis of schools and disciplinary infractions in a large school district. *Education and Treatment of Children, 26*(1), 30–51.

Monahan, K. C., VanDerhei, S., Bechtold, J., & Cauffman, E. (2014). From the school yard to the squad car: School discipline, truancy, and arrest. *Journal of Youth and Adolescence, 43*(7), 1110–1122. doi:10.1007/s10964-014-0103-1

Monroe, C. R. (2006a). African American boys and the discipline gap: Balancing educators' uneven hand. *Educational Horizons, 84*, 102–111.

Monroe, C. R. (2006b). Misbehavior or misinterpretation? Closing the discipline gap through cultural synchronization. *Kappa Delta Pi Record, 42*, 161–165.

Moreno, G., & Gaytán, F. X. (2012). Focus on Latino learners: Developing a foundational understanding of Latino cultures to cultivate student success. *Preventing School Failure: Alternative Education for Children and Youth, 57*(1), 7–16.

Morgan, E., Salomon, N., Plotkin, M., & Cohen, R. (2014). *The school discipline consensus report: Strategies from the field to keep students engaged in school and out of the juvenile justice system.* New York: Council of State Governments.

Mrazek, P. J., & Haggerty, R. J. (Eds.). (1994). *Reducing risks for mental disorders: Frontiers for preventive intervention research.* Washington, DC: National Academy Press.

Murray, C., & Greenberg, M. T. (2001). Relationships with teachers and bonds with school: Social emotional adjustment correlates for children with and without disabilities. *Psychology in the Schools, 38*(1), 25–41. doi:10.1002/1520-6807(200101)

National Association for Bilingual Education (NABE). (2002). *Determining appropriate referrals of English language learners to special education: A self-assessment guide for principals.* Arlington, VA: Council for Exceptional Children. Retrieved from http://www.dcsig.org/files/DeterminingAppropriateReferralsOfEnglishLanguageLearnersToSpecialEducation.pdf

O'Connell, M. E., Boat, T., & Warner, K. E. (2009). *Preventing mental, emotional, and behavioral disorders among young people: Progress and possibilities.* Washington, DC: National Academies Press.

Petras, H., Masyn, K. E., Buckley, J. A., Ialongo, N. S., & Sheppard, K. (2011). Who is most at risk for school removal? A multilevel discrete-time survival analysis of individual- and context-level influences. *Journal of Educational Psychology, 103*(1), 223–237.

Porowski, A., O'Conner, R., & Passa, A. (2014). *Disproportionality in school discipline: An assessment of trends in Maryland, 2009–12.* Regional Educational Laboratory Mid-Atlantic; U.S. Department of Education. Retrieved from https://ies.ed.gov/ncee/edlabs/regions/midatlantic/pdf/REL_2014017.pdf

Raible, J., & Irizarry, J. G. (2010). Redirecting the teacher's gaze: Teacher education, youth surveillance and the school-to-prison pipeline. *Teaching and Teacher Education, 26*(5), 1196–1203.

Rausch, M. K., Skiba, R. J., & Simmons, A. B. (2004). *The academic cost of discipline: The relationship between suspension/expulsion and school achievement.* Bloomington, IN: Center for Evaluation and Education Policy, Indiana University.

Richards, H., Brown, A., & Forde, T. (2007). Addressing diversity in schools: Culturally responsive pedagogy. *Teaching Exceptional Children, 23*, 64–68.

Rosenberg, M. S., Westling, D., & McLeskey, J. (2011). *Special education for today's teachers: An introduction* (2nd ed.). New York: Pearson.

Ross, D., Kamman, M., & Coady, M. (2008). Accepting responsibility for the learning of all students. In M. S. Rosenberg, D. Westling, & J. McLeskey (Eds.), *Special education for today's teachers: An introduction.* Upper Saddle River, NJ: Pearson.

Rudd, T. (2014). *Racial disproportionality in school discipline: Implicit bias is heavily implicated.* Retrieved from http://kirwaninstitute.osu.edu/wp-content/uploads/2014/02/racialdisproportionality-schools-02.pdf

Scott, T. M., Alter, P. J., Rosenberg, M., & Borgmeier, C. (2010). Decision-making in secondary and tertiary interventions of school-wide systems of positive behavior support. *Education and Treatment of Children, 33*(4), 513–535. doi:10.1353/etc.2010.0003

Scott, T. M., & Barrett, S. B. (2004). Using staff and student time engaged in disciplinary procedures to evaluate the impact of school-wide PBS. *Journal of Positive Behavior Interventions, 6*, 21–27. doi:10.1177/10983007040060010401

Skiba, R. J., Horner, R. H., Chung, C. G., Karega Rausch, M., May, S. L., & Tobin, T. (2011). Race is not neutral: A national investigation of African American and Latino disproportionality in school discipline. *School Psychology Review, 40*(1), 85–107.

Skiba, R. J., & Knesting, K. (2001). Zero tolerance, zero evidence: An analysis of school disciplinary practice. *New Directions for Youth Development, 2001*(92), 17–43.

Skiba, R. J., Michael, R. S., Nardo, A. C., & Peterson, R. L. (2002). The color of discipline: Sources of racial and gender disproportionality in school punishment. *Urban Review, 34*, 317–342. doi:10.1023/A:1021320817372

Skiba, R. J., Simmons, A. B., Ritter, S., Gibb, A. C., Rausch, M. K., & Cuadrado, J. (2008). Achieving equity in special education: History, status, and current challenges. *Exceptional Children, 74*, 264–288.

Smith, C. D. (2009). Deconstructing the pipeline: Evaluating school-to-prison pipeline equal protection cases through a structural racism framework. *Fordham Urban Law Journal, 36*, 1009.

Sugai, G., Horner, R. H., Dunlap, G., Hieneman, M., Lewis, T. J., Nelson, C. M., ... Ruef, M. (2000). Applying positive behavior support and functional behavioral assessment in schools. *Journal of Positive Behavior Interventions, 2*(3), 131–143.

U.S. Department of Education Office for Civil Rights (2014). *Civil Rights Data Collection. Data snapshot: School discipline* [Data file]. Retrieved from http://ocrdata.ed.gov/Downloads/CRDC-School-Discipline-Snapshot.pdf

Villegas, A. M., & Lucas, T. (2002). Preparing culturally responsive teachers: Rethinking the curriculum. *Journal of Teacher Education, 53*(1), 20–32. doi: 10.1177/0022487102053001003

Vincent, C., Randall, C., Cartledge, G., Tobin, T., & Swain-Bradway, J. (2011). Toward a conceptual integration of cultural responsiveness and schoolwide positive behavior support. *Journal of Positive Behavior Interventions, 13*(4), 219–229. doi:10.1177/1098300711399765

Vincent, C. G., Swain-Bradway, J., Tobin, T. J., & May, S. (2011). Disciplinary referrals for culturally and linguistically diverse students with and without disabilities: Patterns resulting from school-wide positive behavior support. *Exceptionality, 19*(3), 175–190. doi:10.1080/09362835.2011.579936

Wallace, J. M., Jr., Goodkind, S., Wallace, C. M., & Bachman, J. G. (2008). Racial, ethnic, and gender differences in school discipline among U.S. high school students: 1991–2005. *Negro Educational Review, 59*, 47–62.

White House, Office of Press Secretary. (2014). *Presidential Memorandum—Creating and expanding ladders of opportunity for boys and young men of color.* The White House. Retrieved from https://www.whitehouse.gov/the-press-office/2014/02/27/presidential-memorandum-creating-and-expanding-ladders-opportunity-boys-

9 On some types and consequences of after-school activities in low-income neighborhoods

Brad Lian

Children and adolescents spend a substantial amount of their time outside of academic settings. What they do with that time is important and likely contributes to normative development patterns. After-school time, the few hours between when school lets out and dinner time or when parents return home from work, is particularly important because it can be a peak time for delinquency or high-risk behavior (Taheri & Welsh, 2015). This may be especially so in unsupervised settings. Indeed, unsupervised time has consistently been linked to various types of delinquent behavior, substance use, risky sexual behavior, risk of victimization, and dropping out of school (Gottfredson, Gerstenblith, Soule, Womer, & Lu, 2004; Gottfredson, Gottfredson, & Weisman, 2001; Kremer, Maynard, Polanin, Vaughn, & Sarteschi, 2014; Pannoni, 2014; Petit, Bates, Dodge, & Meece, 1999; Rorie, Gottfredson, Cross, Wilson, & Connell, 2011).

In part because of this, and also spurred on by the rise of single-parent and two-income-earning families over the past several decades which has led to an increase in the number of children who are left potentially unsupervised or in latch-key situations, after-school programs have become increasingly common (Fredricks & Simpkins, 2012). Research generally linking involvement in after-school activities and programs to higher levels of self-esteem and prosocial behavior and lower levels of substance use, aggression, and delinquency (Blomfield & Barber, 2011; Durlak, Weissberg, & Pachan, 2010; Fredricks & Eccles, 2006, 2010; Kremer et al., 2014; Kataoka & Vandell, 2013; Lauer et al., 2006; Mahoney, Parente, & Zigler, 2009) is also a major contributor to the growth in such programs, of course.[1] A recent estimate puts the number of elementary, middle, and high school after-school programs at approximately 50,000 (Parsad & Lewis, 2009), with over 2 million youth participating.

---

1 Although these associations are typically small and not always statistically significant, little to no evidence of harmful effects has been reported (Taheri & Welsh, 2015). Setting (school, community, mixture) of the activities, focus (academic, nonacademic, mixed), size, and number of sessions may vary, all of which affect outcomes. Attendance in after-school activities is often sporadic and that may affect results as well. The at-risk may be even less likely to attend.

Such programs are overwhelmingly popular as well; 84% of parents support using public funds for after-school programs (Afterschool Alliance, 2014).

Participation in organized after-school programs may not be an option available to all youth, however. Reasons such as cost (at the school and individual levels), transportation, safety, and home situations may affect participation rates (Burton, Allison, & Obeidallah, 1995; Sanderson & Richards, 2010). For instance, the No Child Left Behind Act targeted after-school program funds toward low-performing schools that were often in high-poverty neighborhoods, the reasoning being that the positive impacts of such programs may be even greater for youth growing up in such environments, where supervision and resources may be lacking and where opportunities for behaviors associated with health risks may be more abundant (Kremer et al., 2014). Participation in such programs may not be an option for many of the youth living in these areas and attending such schools, however, because of the reasons stated earlier. Consequently, working at a paid job, hanging out with friends, or staying home alone may be a primary after-school activity for many, if not a majority of the youth in these situations. Psychosocial and behavioral outcomes are likely associated with these types of activities as well, and are important to consider and better understand if we are to develop or promote healthy activities aimed at improving adolescent health. This may be especially so with respect to African American youth, because they are relatively more likely to grow up in such situations. Unfortunately, African American youth have been understudied in the research on after-school activities (Fredricks & Simpkins, 2012).

This study examines participation levels in several types of after-school activities and outcomes associated with each among African American adolescents growing up in low-income neighborhoods, where opportunities for organized after-school activities may be limited. Types and levels of four after-school activities (participation in organized sports and clubs, working at a job, hanging out with friends, and hanging out alone at home) are assessed by school level (elementary, middle, and high school) and gender because participation rates may vary by such subgroups. Using regression analyses, relationships between the various types and levels of activities and such risk-related attitudes and behaviors as hopelessness, self-worth, substance use, and fighting are then examined. These analyses are based on a community sample of nearly 3,000 adolescents living in extremely economically impoverished neighborhoods (i.e., 73% of the residents in these neighborhoods live below the poverty level) in a midsized southern city in 2011.

METHOD

Sample and procedures

The data used for this study are based on responses from 2,884 adolescents who participated in the 2011 Mobile Youth Survey (MYS). The MYS was a multiple cohort study conducted during summers from 1998 to 2011. Approximately 3,000 African American adolescents between the ages of 10 and 18 participated in the MYS annually. The MYS was designed to identify the life-course trajectories of adolescents living in extreme poverty in the Mobile, Alabama, metropolitan statistical area (MSA). The MSA has a population of over 540,000, but is dominated by the city of Mobile, with a population of approximately 200,000. In 2010, 50.3% of Mobile's population was African American and 22.3% lived in poverty (U.S. Census Bureau, 2010). The median household income was $37,722. Prichard, a city of nearly 25,000, borders Mobile on its north side; in 2010, 36.3% of the residents lived in poverty and 85.8% of its population was African American. Prichard's median household income in 2010 was $23,726 (U.S. Census Bureau, 2010).

The MYS incorporated a community epidemiological approach. That is, it targeted the 13 most impoverished neighborhoods (based on 1990 census data) in the MSA. Studying such a well-defined and homogeneous population is arguably the most effective way to account for several factors that potentially confound other studies of youth outcomes, such as household income, level of neighborhood poverty, and level of neighborhood risk (Kellam, Rebok, Ialongo, & Mayer, 1994; Vaden-Kiernan, Ialongo, Pearson, & Kellam, 1995). Specifically, the neighborhoods, which correspond to single or multiple census tracts or block groups, were home to more than 25,000 residents; the median household income in the neighborhoods (based on the 1990 census) was approximately $5,000, and 73% of the residents in these neighborhoods lived below the poverty level. Although the poverty level in these neighborhoods declined somewhat by 2010, they remained poor by all indicators. Median poverty rates were 57% and 50.7%, in 2000 and 2010, respectively; and the median household income was less than $12,000 in 2000 and $14,651 in 2010. Approximately 95% of residents in these neighborhoods were African American across the census waves, and over 92% of the MYS participants annually reported receiving free or reduced cost lunch at school.

The initial MYS participants (in 1998) were randomly selected, and they were resurveyed during each subsequent year of the project. Each year, a new sample was also recruited from youth who (a) turned 10 during the year or (b) moved into a survey neighborhood during the year. The MYS questionnaire consisted of 406 items covering a number of psychosocial variables adapted from existing scales and modified to reflect the unique characteristics of this sample (e.g., a wide range of ages and heavy use of street vernacular). It also included items concerning risk behaviors (e.g., violence and aggressive behavior, alcohol and drug use, sexual behavior), circumstances (e.g., family structure and function, peer pressure and support), attitudes (about violence, sexuality, and drug and alcohol use), and feelings (e.g., self-worth, hopelessness, future orientation, support from neighborhood). Surveys were administered in group settings (approximately 10–20 youths per administration) at a facility in or nearby the respective neighborhoods (e.g., churches, boys and girls clubs, schools, housing authority facilities). The surveys were in booklet

Table 9.1 Participants by grade level and gender

	All	Males	Females
Elementary school total	881	457	424
Middle school total	742	394	348
High school total	1261	598	663
Overall total	2884	1449	1435

form that the youths filled out by themselves (i.e., self-reports) and took about an hour to complete. Participants were paid $15 for their time.

The MYS was conducted when participants were on summer breaks from school. Participants were categorized as elementary, middle, or high school students based on their responses to the item, "What grade in school will you be in next year?" Elementary school students were defined as those who had just completed the 6th grade or less. Middle school students were defined as those completing the 7th or 8th grades, and so were those who responded that they would be in the 8th grade or 9th grade the next year. High school students were classified in a similar manner; they were those who responded they would be in the 10th, 11th, 12th grade or in college or technical school in the next year. School-level and gender characteristics of the sample are reported in Table 9.1.

Measures

After-school activities

Four after-school activities based on responses to the following items that pertained to how time was spent during the previous school year were assessed:

1. How many hours each week are you involved in organized sports, clubs, or other after-school activities?
2. How many hours each week do you work at a paid job?
3. How many hours each week do you spend hanging out with your friends?
4. How many hours each week do you hang out alone at home?

The response options for the first item (Sports/clubs) were *None, 1–5 hours a week, 6 to 10 hours a week*, and *More than 10 hours a week*. The response options for the latter three items were *None, 1–5 hours a week, 6 to 10 hours a week, 11 to 20 hours a week*, and *More than 20 hours a week*.

Dependent variables: Psychosocial measures

Two psychosocial measures based on items reflecting current (i.e., summer) feelings were assessed, levels of hopelessness, and self-worth. Hopelessness was measured using five items adapted from the Hopelessness Scale for Children (Kazdin, French, Unis, Esveldt-Dawson, & Sherick, 1983). Respondents were asked to agree or disagree with each of five statements (e.g., "All I see ahead of me are bad things, not good things" and "I never get what I want, so it's dumb to want anything"). A sixth statement ("I do not expect to live a very long life") based on low expectations of survival among many inner-city adolescents (e.g., DuRant, Cadenhead, Pendergrast, Slavens, & Linder, 1994) was also added. Responses were summed to create a Brief Hopelessness Scale that ranged between 0 and 6, with low scores reflecting low hopelessness and high scores reflecting high hopelessness ($M = 1.07$, $SD = 1.65$). The internal reliability was adequate (Cronbach's alpha = .78).

Self-worth was an additive scale adopted from Harter (1982) based on nine sets of statements where respondents were asked to choose the statement that best describes him or her. Sample pairs of statements include (a) I'm usually unhappy with myself or (b) I'm usually happy with myself; and (a) I like the kind of person I am or (b) I don't like the kind of person I am. The scale ranges from 0 to 9 with an alpha of .61 ($M = 6.67$, $SD = 1.96$), with higher scores indicating a greater sense of self-worth.

Behavioral measures

The behaviors assessed concerned fighting and getting drunk or high. Following Browne, Clubb, Aubrecht, and Jackson (2001), multiple questions were asked about each behavior during increasingly short intervals (e.g., Have you ever gotten into a physical fight? During the past three months, have you gotten into a physical fight? During the past month, have you gotten into a physical fight?). The series of questions were combined into single recency–frequency indices, with higher scores reflecting more recent and higher activity levels.

Descriptive statistics for the dependent measures are reported in Table 9.2. Statistically significant gender differences are evident for each outcome, with males, on average, reporting higher levels of hopelessness, fighting, and substance usage, and lower levels of self-worth than females.

Analysis plan

Differences at the subgroup level can be obscured by aggregate data, so first, descriptive statistics regarding levels of participation for the four after-school activities by school level (elementary, middle, and high school) and gender are reported. Using regression analyses, relationships between the various types and levels of activities and such risk-related attitudes and behaviors as hopelessness, self-worth, substance use, and fighting are then examined. The regressions are also conducted by gender and school level because the outcomes considered may vary at these levels as well, and the large sample size of the MYS allows for analyses at such levels, which best controls for potential confounders associated with both.

Table 9.2 Descriptives regarding the dependent variables

	All (n = 2840–2871)[a]	Males (n = 1415–1446)	Females (n = 1410–1428)	Male–Female difference
	Mean (SD)	Mean (SD)	Mean (SD)	t
Hopelessness (range 0–6)	1.07 (1.65)	1.30 (1.79)	0.83 (1.45)	7.74**
Self-worth (range 0–9)	6.67 (1.96)	6.49 (1.94)	6.86 (1.96)	–5.10**
Fighting (range 0–5)	2.10 (1.66)	2.31 (1.66)	1.89 (1.63)	6.74**
Getting drunk or high (range 0–7)	1.46 (2.49)	1.73 (2.66)	1.20 (2.29)	5.69**

a Sample sizes vary based on measure assessed.
**$p \leq .01$

RESULTS

Involvement in after-school activities

Involvement in after-school activities by school type and overall are reported in Table 9.3, with the corresponding percentages by gender reported in Table 9.4.

Sports/clubs

Approximately 40% of adolescents reported not participating in any after-school sports or clubs. Although the level of no involvement increased slightly with age, a consistent 25% to 30% of the students reported being involved at least 6 hours per week across school type.

Table 9.3 After-school participation percentages by school level (all participants)

		School level			
Activity	*Hrs/week*	*Elementary*	*Middle*	*High*	*All levels*
Sports/clubs	0	35.0%	35.4%	43.4%	38.8%
	1–5	39.1%	34.5%	27.3%	32.7%
	6–10	14.6%	15.3%	15.5%	15.2%
	>10	11.3%	14.8%	13.9%	13.3%
	n	879	741	1256	2876
Paid job	0	78.0%	77.4%	72.2%	75.3%
	1–5	12.3%	12.2%	8.5%	10.6%
	6–10	5.0%	4.4%	5.9%	5.3%
	11–20	2.6%	3.2%	6.1%	4.3%
	>20	2.2%	2.8%	7.4%	4.6%
	n	877	745	1258	2880
With friends	0	8.8%	5.9%	11.3%	9.2%
	1–5	47.1%	30.5%	23.9%	32.7%
	6–10	22.5%	26.3%	24.4%	24.3%
	11–20	10.4%	14.9%	17.8%	14.8%
	>20	11.2%	22.3%	22.7%	19.1%
	n	881	742	1261	2884
Home alone	0	39.5%	29.2%	20.1%	28.4%
	1–5	32.9%	37.7%	33.2%	34.3%
	6–10	14.8%	16.7%	21.3%	18.2%
	11–20	5.7%	8.2%	14.7%	10.3%
	>20	7.1%	8.2%	10.7%	9.0%
	n	880	741	1259	2880

Table 9.4 After-school participation percentages by gender and school level

	Hrs/wk	Males				Females			
		E.S.	M.S.	H.S.	All	E.S.	M.S.	H.S.	All
Sports/clubs	0	27.2%	27.5%	34.9%	30.4%	43.2%	44.3%	51.2%	47.2%
	1–5	42.6%	34.1%	27.3%	34.0%	35.3%	34.8%	27.0%	31.3%
	6–10	18.3%	20.1%	19.0%	19.0%	10.7%	10.1%	12.3%	11.3%
	>10	12.0%	18.3%	18.8%	16.5%	10.7%	10.9%	9.5%	10.2%
	n	460	393	596	1449	419	348	660	1427
Paid job	0	72.1%	70.6%	67.5%	69.8%	84.4%	85.3%	76.6%	81.0%
	1–5	16.3%	14.6%	10.7%	13.5%	7.8%	9.2%	6.2%	7.4%
	6–10	5.1%	5.8%	7.0%	6.1%	5.0%	2.9%	5.0%	4.5%
	11–20	3.5%	5.0%	7.2%	5.4%	1.7%	1.2%	5.1%	3.1%
	>20	3.1%	4.0%	7.5%	5.2%	1.2%	1.4%	7.1%	4.0%
	n	455	398	597	1450	422	347	661	1430
With friends	0	6.6%	6.1%	11.0%	8.3%	11.1%	5.5%	11.3%	9.8%
	1–5	41.8%	28.7%	23.7%	30.8%	53.1%	32.5%	24.0%	34.6%
	6–10	26.0%	25.6%	20.4%	23.6%	18.4%	27.3%	28.2%	25.1%
	11–20	12.5%	17.3%	19.6%	16.7%	8.3%	12.4%	16.0%	12.8%
	>20	13.1%	22.3%	25.3%	20.6%	9.2%	22.4%	20.5%	17.6%
	n	457	394	598	1449	424	348	663	1435
Home alone	0	34.7%	25.6%	19.8%	26.1%	45.0%	32.9%	20.2%	30.6%
	1–5	34.7%	41.5%	35.0%	36.7%	31.0%	33.5%	31.4%	31.8%
	6–10	17.0%	16.5%	22.8%	19.2%	12.1%	17.1%	20.2%	17.1%
	11–20	6.6%	8.4%	13.6%	9.9%	4.5%	8.1%	15.7%	10.6%
	>20	7.0%	8.1%	8.9%	8.1%	7.3%	8.4%	12.4%	9.9%
	n	458	395	597	1450	422	346	662	1430

Males reported more involvement than females at each school level, and in middle and high school were about twice as likely to be involved at least 6 hours per week than their female counterparts. Over 50% of high school females reported no involvement in after-school sports or clubs.

Paid job

Most students (72%–78%) reported not having a paid job, as one would expect, and the percentage reporting so was fairly consistent across school levels. Also as expected, high schoolers were over twice as likely to report working for a wage over 11 hours per week than elementary or middle schoolers. Still, though, approximately 25% of the students across school levels reported working for pay at least some of the time during the school year. Males generally reported higher levels of paid employment than females, but percentages with respect to working for pay over 11 hours per week were similar for the genders during the high school period (14.7% for males and 12.2% for females).

Hanging out with friends

Most students (approximately 90%) reported hanging out at least some of the time with friends after school. The time spent with friends was more limited (0–5 hours per week) during the elementary school period; however, 55.9% of the elementary students reported hanging out 5 or less hours per week with their friends, compared to about 36% for the middle and high schoolers. Middle and high school students are much more likely to hang out with friends more than 11 hours per week than those attending elementary school. Percentages and trends within and across school levels were similar by gender.

Hanging out alone at home

Reported time spent alone at home increased as school level increased. Females in elementary school reported being the most likely to spend zero time home alone after school (45%). Approximately twice as many high schoolers reported spending at least 11 hours per week hanging out alone at home than those in elementary school, at 25.4% and 12.8%, respectively. Similarly, elementary students were about twice as likely to report never hanging out alone at home than their high school counterparts, at 39.5% and 20.1%, respectively. Percentages and trends were essentially similar by gender.

Involvement and outcomes

Overall, as can be seen in Tables 9.5 and 9.6, more statistically significant (i.e., $p < .05$) relationships were reported between the activities and outcomes assessed with respect to males (Table 9.5) than females (Table 9.6). Gender differences with respect to after-school activities and self-worth were especially evident,

Table 9.5 Regression results for males

	Hopelessness	Self-worth	Getting drunk/ high	Fighting
			b (SE)	
Elementary school				
Sports/clubs	−0.062 (0.092)	0.009 (0.104)	−0.232 (0.069)**	0.157 (0.089)
Paid job	0.506 (0.094)**	−0.306 (0.104)**	0.155 (0.064)*	0.082 (0.091)
With friends	0.064 (0.076)	−0.169 (0.085)*	0.340 (0.057)**	0.258 (0.073)**
Home alone	0.046 (0.071)	−0.031 (0.080)	0.092 (0.060)	0.047 (0.069)
adj R^2	.06	.03	.04	.05
Middle school				
Sports/clubs	0.135 (0.081)	0.048 (0.088)	−0.307 (0.086)**	0.037 (0.082)
Paid job	0.235 (0.081)**	−0.071 (0.088)	0.052 (0.078)	0.213 (0.082)**
With friends	−0.084 (0.068)	−0.116 (0.074)	0.281 (0.071)**	0.092 (0.069)
Home alone	0.069 (0.072)	−0.058 (0.078)	0.059 (0.078)	0.109 (0.073)
adj R^2	.03	.01	.02	.03
High school				
Sports/clubs	−0.147 (0.067)*	0.359 (0.072)**	−0.397 (0.11)**	−0.177 (0.059)**
Paid job	0.084 (0.058)	−0.136 (0.063)*	−0.021 (0.095)	0.103 (0.052)*
With friends	−0.216 (0.055)	−0.012 (0.060)	0.364 (0.091)	0.067 (0.049)
Home alone	−0.043 (0.062)	0.100 (0.067)	0.039 (0.103)	0.075 (0.055)
adj R^2	.04	.04	.04	.02

*$p \leq .05$
**$p \leq .01$

in that none of the after-school activities was related to level of self-worth at any school level among the females, while 2 of the 4 activities were associated with self-worth among males in elementary and high school. The results also indicate that outcomes associated with middle school students are difficult to predict, at least with respect to the variables used in this study.

Sports/clubs

Overall, after-school involvement in sports/clubs was more important for males than females with respect to the outcomes assessed in this study, and the effects were always beneficial or protective. Gender differences related to involvement in sports/clubs are particularly marked among those in high school, where such involvement was significantly associated with lower levels of hopelessness and fighting, and higher levels of self-worth for males but to none of these outcomes among females. Sports/clubs involvement was negatively related to getting drunk or high for males at each school level and for females in middle school.

Table 9.6 Regression results for females

	Hopelessness	Self-worth	Getting drunk/ high	Fighting
			b (SE)	
Elementary school				
Sports/clubs	0.075 (0.080)	0.041 (0.103)	–0.162 (0.061)**	0.002 (0.091)
Paid job	0.381 (0.108)**	–0.015 (0.139)	0.127 (0.06)*	0.122 (0.123)
With friends	–0.014 (0.070)	–0.078 (0.090)	0.539 (0.048)**	0.257 (0.080)**
Home alone	0.036 (0.063)	–0.089 (0.081)	0.022 (0.047)	0.018 (0.071)
adj R^2	.04	<.01	0.09	.02
Middle school				
Sports/clubs	–0.026 (0.080)	0.148 (0.115)	–0.139 (0.081)	0.120 (0.096)
Paid job	0.19 (0.112)	–0.239 (0.161)	0.085 (0.073)	–0.086 (0.135)
With friends	0.050 (0.061)	–0.085 (0.088)	0.538 (0.062)**	0.141 (0.074)
Home alone	0.008 (0.062)	0.027 (0.089)	–0.077 (0.062)	–0.022 (0.075)
adj R^2	<.01	<.01	.07	.01
High school				
Sports/clubs	–0.038 (0.056)	0.091 (0.077)	–0.085 (0.102)	0.033 (0.060)
Paid job	0.021 (0.045)	0.065 (0.062)	–0.010 (0.082)	0.080 (0.048)
With friends	–0.040 (0.043)	–0.106 (0.059)	0.536 (0.078)**	0.172 (0.046)**
Home alone	0.103 (0.043)*	0.002 (0.059)	–0.090 (0.078)	–0.097 (0.046)*
adj R^2	.01	<.01	.06	.02

*$p \leq .05$
**$p \leq .01$

Paid job

Hours spent working at a paid job each week was consistently related to negative outcomes, especially among males. For instance, it was associated with higher levels of hopelessness and getting drunk or high, and lower levels of self-worth for boys in elementary school; and with higher levels of fighting to those in middle and high school. It was also associated with higher levels of hopelessness and lower levels of self-worth among males in middle and high school, respectively. Hours at a paid job was also positively related to hopelessness and getting drunk or high among females in elementary school, but was not associated in a statistically significant manner with any of the outcomes assessed for females in middle or high school.

Hanging out with friends

Overall, time spent hanging out with friends was related to several of the outcomes assessed for students in elementary and high school, and none of these relationships were beneficial or positive for youth. Specifically, time spent hanging out with friends was statistically significant in relation to getting drunk or high for males and females at all school levels. It was also positively associated with fighting for both sexes in elementary school and for females in high school, and to higher levels of hopelessness and lower levels of self-worth for high school and elementary school males, respectively.

Hanging out alone at home

Hours spent hanging out alone at home was not significantly related to any of the outcomes for males, regardless of school level. Relationships between it and the outcomes for females were limited as well, with the exceptions being its positive relationship to hopelessness and negative relationship to fighting among those in high school. Hours spent alone at home was unimportant for elementary and middle school youth with respect to the outcomes assessed here.

DISCUSSION

Understanding the nature and extent of after-school activities and the outcomes associated with them is critical if we are to develop or promote healthy activities aimed at improving adolescent health. Doing so is easier said than done, however, because such activities and the outcomes associated with them vary by grade levels, gender, location, and resource availability, among other things. Studies need to account for such variation or they risk being irrelevant and ungeneralizable.

The findings reported here are based on data at the school level and by gender from an understudied yet important population: African American adolescents growing up in economically impoverished neighborhoods. This is an important population because many after-school programs are targeted toward and developed with such youth in mind.

With respect to the four after-school activities examined here, school-level and gender differences were evident across activities and activity levels. Males consistently reported higher levels of involvement than females in each activity assessed. Trends regarding hours of involvement over time (i.e., from elementary to middle to high school) were similar for both genders.

Many have suggested that youth may have more freedom to select how they spend their after-school time as they age (Fredricks & Simpkins, 2012; Posner & Vandell, 1995; Rorie et al., 2011; Scarr & McCartney, 1983). That appears to be the case here. The percentage of responses associated with zero time spent in activities increased with school level; for instance, more youth choose to hang out alone at home and to be uninvolved in sports/clubs over time. They also choose to spend more time with their friends. It may also be the case that there is a shortage of attractive after-school activities in these underresourced neighborhoods. The vast majority (70% of the males and

81% of the females) of the high school youth in these neighborhoods reported not having a paid job, and only 10% to 15% of them reported working over 10 hours a week, so attractive after-school activities or alternative activities for African American high school youth would seem to be in demand.

Perhaps local apprenticeship offerings would be attractive to both youth and the community-at-large. A model program in this regard may be the After School Matters (ASM) initiative developed by Barton Hirsch and Larry Hedges at Northwestern University. For the past several years, ASM has provided apprenticeships (approximately 90 hours each fall and spring) to adolescents in the Chicago area in collaboration with local organizations and human resource managers from area businesses who are relied upon to help identify local workforce needs. Such apprenticeships are intended to help encourage students to graduate and prepare them for their next steps in life.

Outcomes associated with the after-school activities examined here varied by age and gender as well, and were particularly difficult to predict for the middle and high school females. There was little evidence that after-school activities were more important with respect to the outcomes assessed for younger youth than for the older ones. The middle school period was different than the other two periods, however, in that statistically significant associations between after-school activities and psychosocial and behavioral outcomes were rarer. Middle school is a very dynamic developmental time for youth, physically and socially. It is a period associated with relatively immature capacities for self-control (e.g., sensation seeking and impulsivity) and thus higher levels of risk taking behavior (Steinberg et al., 2008). Getting drunk or high and fighting, for instance, may simply be more random or situational events without patterns in many instances in middle school, and self-worth and hopelessness may be explained by other factors or perhaps sporadic yet significant events than were assessed here.

Interestingly, time spent working at paid jobs was typically related to negative outcomes, especially for younger youth. In low socioeconomic status neighborhoods such as these, African American adolescents who work may be doing so to help support their families. Those who are working may feel resentful or disappointed because they have to work while their counterparts do not, which may lead to negative outcomes.

Time spent hanging out with friends was always positively associated with substance use and sometimes to increased levels of fighting. Presumably, a lot of time spent with friends is also time without adult supervision. Supervision has been shown to be important in most research on after-school activities, so the findings reported here arguably corroborate this and suggest it may be an important protective factor for youth development.

Positive outcomes were also always associated with participation levels in sports/clubs at the high school level for males. Such youth have higher levels of self-worth and lower levels of hopelessness, substance use, and fighting. Perhaps such participation is an indicator of positive motivation or wanting to escape the situation at home or in the neighborhood, or of their motivation to leave the area or to meet new folks or to seek healthy adventures or novel situations. In any event, these findings suggest that males who choose to participate in such activities at the high school level are likely on a healthier developmental trajectory than their counterparts who do not.

This study has several limitations. It is based on self-reports from youth growing up in poverty in a single midsized city in the south. Although we surveyed youth from several neighborhoods within the city to best represent this population, generalizability may be a concern. Moreover, only four of a potential multitude of after-school activities were assessed. And the items used to assess these four were very general. The sport or type of club may matter, for instance, and "friends" can be interpreted as any group of more than two individuals, and there may be a difference between 2 and 10. Paid jobs may also be interpreted differently by elementary school youth than high school students. Many of these youth may do chores or babysitting after school, so the absence of paid jobs or employment may not necessarily mean the absence of some type of work. Finally, although the direction of causality in the relationships reported may still be unclear, even though the school-activities data were retrospective in covering previous school year, the dependent measures were based on current (i.e., summertime) attitudes and feelings because interpretations can vary.

In conclusion, African American youth spend their after-school time in a variety of ways. Many high school youth in low-income neighborhoods spend a considerable amount of that time hanging out with friends. Opportunities to channel some of this after-school time toward constructive, productive, and potentially creative endeavors seem to exist. Offering or developing some, or more, attractive after-school opportunities, perhaps in conjunction with local businesses, would likely be beneficial at the individual and community level.

REFERENCES

Afterschool Alliance. (2014). *America after 3PM: Afterschool programs in demand.* http://afterschoolalliance.org/documents/AA3PM-2014/AA3PM_National_Report.pdf

Blomfield, C., & Barber, B. (2011). Developmental experiences during extracurricular activities and Australian adolescents' self-concept: Particularly important for youth from disadvantaged schools. *Journal of Youth and Adolescence, 40*, 582–594.

Browne, D. C., Clubb, P. A., Aubrecht, A. M. B., & Jackson, M. (2001). Minority health risk behaviors: An introduction to research on sexually transmitted diseases, violence, pregnancy prevention and substance use. *Journal of Maternal and Child Health, 5*(4), 215–224. http://doi.org/10.1023/A:1013077404562

Burton, L. M., Allison, K. W., & Obeidallah, D. (1995). Social context and adolescence: Perspective on development among inner-city African-American teens. In L. C. Crockett & A. C. Crouter (Eds.), *Pathways through adolescence* (pp. 119–138). Hillsdale, NJ: Erlbaum.

DuRant, R. H., Cadenhead, C., Pendergrast, R. A., Slavens, G., & Linder, C. W. (1994). Factors associated with the use of violence among urban black adolescents. *American Journal of Public Health, 84*(4), 612–617. http://doi.org/10.2105/AJPH.84.4.612

Durlak, J. A., Weissberg, R. P., & Pachan, M. (2010). A meta-analysis of after-school programs that seek to promote personal social skills in children and adolescents. *American Journal of Community Psychology*, *45*, 294–309.

Fredricks, J. A., & Eccles, J. S. (2006). Is extracurricular participation associated with beneficial outcomes: Concurrent and longitudinal relations? *Developmental Psychology*, *42*, 698–713. doi:10.1037/0012-1649.42.4.698

Fredricks, J., & Eccles, J. S. (2010). Breadth of extracurricular participation and adolescent adjustment among African-American and European-American youth. *Journal of Research on Adolescence*, *20*(2), 307–333.

Fredricks, J. A., & Simpkins, S. D. (2012). Promoting positive youth development through organized after-school activities: Taking a closer look at participation of ethnic minority youth. *Child Development Perspectives*, *6*(3), 280–287.

Gottfredson, D. C., Gerstenblith, S. A., Soule, D., Womer, S. C., & Lu, S. (2004). Do after school programs reduce delinquency? *Journal of Prevention Science*, *5*(4), 253–266.

Gottfredson, D. C., Gottfredson, G. D., & Weisman, S. A. (2001). The timing of delinquent behavior and its implications for after-school programs. *Criminology & Public Policy*, *1*, 61–86.

Harter, S. (1982). The perceived competence scale for children. *Child Development*, *53*(1), 87–97. doi:10.2307/1129640

Kataoka, S., & Vandell, D. L. (2013). Quality of afterschool activities and relative change in adolescent functioning over two years. *Applied Developmental Science*, *17*(3), 123–134. doi:10.1080/10888691.2013.804375

Kazdin, A. E., French, N. H., Unis, A. S., Esveldt-Dawson, K., & Sherick, R. B. (1983). Hopelessness, depression, and suicidal intent among psychiatrically disturbed inpatient children. *Journal of Consulting and Clinical Psychology*, *51*(4), 504–510. http://doi.org/10.1037/0022-006X.51.4.504

Kellam, S. G., Rebok, G. W., Ialongo, N., & Mayer, L. S. (1994). The course and malleability of aggressive behavior from early first grade into middle school: Results of a developmental epidemiologically-based preventive trial. *Journal of Child Psychology and Psychiatry*, *35*(2), 259–281. http://doi.org/10.1111/j.1469-7610.1994.tb01161.x

Kremer, K. P., Maynard, B. R., Polanin, J. R., Vaughn, M. G., & Sarteschi, C. M. (2014). Effects of after-school programs with at-risk youth on attendance and externalizing behaviors: A systematic review and meta-analysis. *Journal of Youth and Adolescence*, *44*(3), 616–636.

Lauer, P. A., Akiba, M., Wilkerson, S. B., Apthorp, H. S., Snow, D., & Martin-Glenn, M. L. (2006). Out-of-school-time programs: A meta-analysis of effects for at-risk students. *Review of Educational Research*, *76*(2), 275–313.

Mahoney, J. L., Parente, M. E., & Zigler, E. F. (2009). Afterschool programs in America: Origins, growth, popularity, and politics. *Journal of Youth Development*, *4*, 25–44.

Pannoni, A. (2014, November 3). Students who participate in after-school programs stay on track to graduate high school, one report revealed. *US News & World Report*. Retrieved from http://www.usnews.com/education/blogs/high-school-notes/2014/11/03/after-school-programs-can-help-teens-at-risk-of-dropping-out

Parsad, B., & Lewis, L. (2009). *After-school programs in public elementary schools (NCES 2009-043)*. Washington, DC: National Center for Education Statistics.

Petit, G. S., Bates, J. F., Dodge, K. A., & Meece, D. W. (1999). The impact of after-school peer contact on early adolescent externalizing problems moderated by parental monitoring, perceived neighborhood safety, and prior adjustment. *Child Development*, *70*, 768–778. doi:10.1111/1467-8624.00055

Posner, J. K., & Vandell, D. L. (1999). After-school activities and the development of low-income urban children: A longitudinal study. *Developmental Psychology, 35*(3), 868–879.

Rorie, M., Gottfredson, D. C., Cross, A., Wilson, D., & Connell, N. M. (2011). Structure and deviancy training in after-school programs. *Journal of Adolescence, 34*, 105–117.

Sanderson, R., & Richards, M. (2010). The after-school needs and resources of a low-income urban community: Surveying youth and parents for community change. *American Journal of Community Psychology, 45*, 430–440.

Scarr, S., & McCartney, K. (1983). How people make their own environments: A theory of genotype-environment effects. *Child Development, 64*, 1333–1353.

Steinberg, L., Albert, D., Cauffman, E., Banich, M., Graham, S., & Woolard, J. (2008). Age differences in sensation seeking and impulsivity as indexed by behavior and self-report: Evidence for a dual systems model. *Developmental Psychology, 44*(6), 1764–1778.

Taheri, S. A., & Welsh, B. C. (2015). After-school programs for delinquency prevention a systematic review and meta-analysis. *Youth Violence and Juvenile Justice.* doi:1541204014567542

U.S. Census Bureau. (2010). *State and county quickfacts.* Retrieved from U.S. Census Bureau, http://quickfacts.census.gov/qfd/states/01/0162496.html

Vaden-Kiernan, N., Ialongo, N. S., Pearson, J., & Kellam, S. (1995). Household family structure and children's aggressive behavior: A longitudinal study of urban elementary school children. *Journal of Abnormal Child Psychology, 23*(5), 553–568. http://doi.org/10.1007/BF01447661

Epilogue

The linkages between a student's health and a student's ability to learn have been well established. Former Surgeon General Jocelyn Elders, MD, once said, "You can't educate a child who isn't healthy, and you can't keep children healthy who are not educated." A concerted focus only on the educational and medical needs of the child is not enough. Children who are sick stay home, and children at home cannot learn if they are not in school, leading to increased dropout rates among other educational outcomes. However, an understanding of this concept is just the beginning of understanding how education and public health are inextricably linked. In light of this, this book examined health disparities and education inequities simultaneously and moves beyond a basic understanding of health and education. It examined the important connection between education and health in K–12 school programs.

Linking Health and Education for African American Students' Success presented the opportunity to examine health disparities and education inequities simultaneously. The structural inequalities that lead to reduced academic attainment mirror the social determinants of health. Education is one of the most powerful determinants of health, and disparities in educational achievement as a result of structural inequalities closely track disparities in health. These disparities lead to both substandard healthcare and reduced academic attainment among children from underserved minorities in the United States, especially African Americans. *Linking Health and Education for African American Students' Success* discussed how this may result in children with poorer mental health outcomes, higher school-dropout rates, increased risks of arrests and incarceration, higher rates of chronic diseases and mortality, and overall diminished opportunities for success. However, it also offered solutions for how to improve outcomes for children in K–12.

Disparities in health status and access to health care between different racial, ethnic, and socioeconomic groups in the United States are a demonstrated fact. There is increased awareness about health disparities and attempts to reduce them. Likewise, there is abundant documented evidence of the marked educational gaps between different racial, ethnic, and socioeconomic groups. The education gap begins before children go to kindergarten, and the gap widens as children continue their schooling. The end results are low achievement and high school dropout rates among minority populations. Just like in the case of health, there have been numerous efforts to increase awareness about these problems and attempts to reduce educational inequities. For both health disparities and educational inequities, initiatives have included designing, testing, and training on selective interventions, and also promoting progressive policy making at local, state, and national levels to attempt to reduce their impact on children and youth. It is proposed that these are not two distinct problems; instead they are both the result of structural inequalities that must be addressed in order to improve the lives of children of color in the United States.

What is already known about the intersection of these two problems? Health problems affect children's educational achievement both directly and indirectly. New knowledge of brain development and early learning has shown that children's early experiences can have an effect on their early learning trajectories (Shonkoff, 2010). One well-known example is lead poisoning, which can lead to cognition and behavior problems in school throughout a student's academic career. Racial differences in health conditions and in maternal health and behavior may account for up to 25% of the racial gap in school readiness (Currie, 2005). Currently 1 in 5 children in the United States live in poverty, including 1 in 3 Latino and African American children (Macartney, 2011). Minority children living in poverty are not only more likely to have particular health conditions but they also are less likely to be treated for them.

The evidence indicates that high-risk populations for health problems are usually also high risk for educational problems and vice versa. Thus, beyond their particular characteristics, health disparities and education inequities seem to be two related outcomes of the same mother-problem: socioeconomic (structural) inequalities. It is known that socioeconomic inequalities affect racial and ethnic minorities harder than the majority population. Recent reports show scarce progress in reducing these inequalities. Specifically, the United States is failing to make sufficient progress toward the Healthy People 2020 goal of reducing health disparities. From both scientific and technical standpoints, it is necessary to continue elucidating the best practices to address child health disparities and education inequities, with emphasis on promotional and preventive approaches, rather than remedial ones.

Residents of disadvantaged neighborhoods experience reduced access to jobs, poorer quality schools, higher crime, higher rates of environmental exposures such as lead and tobacco, less capacity to build financial assets, and erosion of social cohesion, with negative impacts on health. The impact of neighborhood disadvantage is particularly profound during childhood. Research on adverse childhood experiences, brain development, and toxic stress are uncovering the mechanisms by which neighborhood exposures, such as unsafe streets or unstable and poor quality housing, can get "under the skin," with lifelong impacts on health. Adverse experiences produce stress responses and increased allostatic load, in turn influencing gene expression and brain development. These effects create a multigenerational cycle of place-based disadvantage. Ensuring healthy child development requires reducing children's exposure to neighborhood stressors, increasing supportive factors in the neighborhood, and nurturing good family and caregiving functioning.

There are a number of ways that education and health agencies can best collaborate to improve African American students' health and chances for academic achievement. Many of them have been outlined throughout this book. Chief among them has been the need to provide or expand services that support at-risk students, those that have barriers to learning that may be created by health conditions, exposure to violence or trauma, or instability or stress in the community or at home. Wraparound services have been shown to provide benefit to children, especially those who are low-income, chronically absent, homeless, or otherwise at risk for failure in school. Trauma or maltreatment, as has been outlined throughout the book, can negatively affect brain development. Coordinated services that address trauma are likely to promote brain development and improve learning ability. Health and education agencies working together to use federal funding, such as Medicaid, can connect students and families with the necessary health care and related support services (e.g., housing, transportation) to address the academic and physical, mental, and behavioral needs of these students in order for them to achieve success.

It is expected that *Linking Health and Education for African American Students' Success* will appeal to educated lay persons, academics, and practitioners in the fields of public health, education, and social work, especially those who have an interest in social justice issues and child well-being. It may be most relevant to those in these fields who conduct intervention research within schools, especially those in which children of color are predominate. It is hoped that upon completing this book readers will come away with a comprehensive understanding of the structural inequities that have an effect on child well-being and come away with the passion to begin to address these inequities. The essays contained in *Linking Health and Education for African American Students' Success* aimed to describe the social determinants of academic success with a principal focus on public health considerations that range broadly to include dietary factors to access to quality healthcare. This work was extrapolated from the literature on social determinants of health and an exhaustive analysis of the extant literature on educational inequities all in relation to well-being and resilience in African American youth. It also included real-world discussion of real-world research currently being conducted to support African American students with a particular focus on academic achievement and success. This research suggests that interventions such as a schoolwide system of support, which includes data-based decision making, professional development for school staff on cultural proficiency; and, culturally sensitive classroom management, all hold promise as effective strategies for improving academic outcomes for African American children and youth.

REFERENCES

Currie, J. M. (2005). Health disparities and gaps in school readiness. *The Future of Children, 15*(1), 117–138.

Macartney, S. (2011). *Child poverty in the United States 2009 and 2010: Selected race groups and Hispanic origin*. U.S. Census Bureau. Retrieved from http://www.census .gov/prod/2011pubs/acsbr10-05.pdf

Shonkoff, J. P. (2010). Building a new biodevelopmental framework to guide the future of early childhood policy. *Child Development, 81*(1), 357–367.

Index

Page numbers followed by f, t, and n indicate figures, tables, and notes, respectively.